Praise

"My friend Rhonda Milner has just made a significant contribution to the minds, hearts, and imaginations of those who savor her clear, compelling, and convincing portraits of the truth, goodness, and beauty of the Creator of all things. *The Signature of God* skillfully combines scientific, imaginative, creative, poetic, and devotional motifs to craft a rich and inviting portrait of the boundless wonders of the creation in which we are immersed. On every order of magnitude, nature points beyond itself to moral and spiritual truth to those who have the eyes to see and the ears to hear. The radiant glory of the Father, the boundless wonders of Yeshua, the God-man, and the power and comfort of the Spirit are evident in this rich collection of truths, stories, marvels, and images."

—**Dr. Kenneth Boa,** ThM, PhD, DPhil, President of Reflections Ministries, Omnibus Media Ministries, and Trinity House Publishers; author of *Conformed to His Image* and *Life in the Presence of God*

"Dallas Willard often said, 'Don't ever let anyone tell you anything bad about God.' For many years, this simple statement has served as an important heresy check for me and as an invitation to think more magnificently about the Trinity. Reading *The Signature of God* is a wonderful way to marvel at how the greatness of God is revealed in both the natural order and in humanity. Rhonda Milner does a masterful job of weaving together stories from her childhood, observations from her medical training, heartfelt experiences as a mother, and keen theological insights to produce a tapestry of the Goodness, Beauty, and Compassion of the One who created us, and as unbelievable as this may sound, in his own Image."

—**Gary W. Moon,** MDiv, PhD, Founding Executive Director of the Martin Institute for Christianity and Culture and Dallas Willard Center, Westmont College, and the Renovaré Institute; author of *Becoming Dallas Willard* and *Apprenticeship with Jesus*

"On a work of art, the signature and date, as inscribed by the artist, not only provide information, but, in many cases, enhance the value of the work. Dr. Rhonda Dawes Milner makes us think far beyond the confines of a gallery or a library. By creating the Universe, Almighty God produced the greatest masterpiece of all time, but He left no room for a physical signature. Instead, He created, as part of His Universe, the Earth and its inhabitants. *The Signature of God* reminds us who dwell on Earth that we are surrounded every day by the wondrous works of God, works which exemplify that there is a loving God who created us and protects us. Therefore, God's Masterpiece requires no physical signature. The lives of His creatures interweave into a beautiful signature, which is skillfully and eloquently illustrated in this book."

—**RICHARD S. COLVIN,** MD FACR, Professor Emeritus at
Emory University School of Medicine

"*The Signature of God* is a work of creative alchemy. As a devotional writer, Rhonda contemplates the natural landscape and sees the very presence of God himself. All of nature becomes sacramental to her: an outward and visible sign of the invisible grace of the Beloved. With each page, Rhonda humbly invites us to explore the Divine imprint on every living thing. Let us journey with her."

—**KATHRYN C. LARISEY,** MS, LPC, CPCS, DCC, Licensed Professional Counselor,
Certified Professional Counselor Supervisor, and Spiritual Director

"If you've ever wondered about the existence of God or His love for you, let Rhonda Milner put your mind at ease. In *The Signature of God*, she details her own quest to identify and document God's intimate presence in her life and His personal activity in the world He created. Through her keen observations of nature and her poetic images, Rhonda offers you and I the opportunity to explore how God the Creator displays His character in the physical realm. She then shows us how He makes Himself known in intimate, personal ways to every individual. Rhonda has experienced the love and comfort of the Father through trial and triumph and in this book, you'll learn how to see Him in everything you encounter in life. God healed Rhonda's need to experience His presence. Perhaps He will use this book to heal yours."

—**NANCY MCGUIRK,** Founder and Lead Teacher of Women's Community Bible
Study and author of *My New Life in Christ*, *Rest Assured*, and *To Live Is Christ*

"*The Signature of God* is not a book about religion and faith alone. It is that and much more. Rhonda Milner brilliantly brings in science, medicine, the arts, music, and geography into her discussion and builds a strong and convincing case that all of what we see and feel around us in this world and in everyday life are signal of God's ever-presence and omnipotence. This is a beautiful book, filled with stories about faith, religion, and science, presented together as one seamless continuum. Irrespective of the differing perceptions we may each have of a supreme being or creator of heaven and earth, this book will bring joy to those who read it."

—OMAR M. LATTOUF, MD, PhD, Cardiothoracic Surgeon and Professor of Surgery at Emory University School of Medicine; author of *Heartfelt Stories: The Life of a Heart Surgeon*

"In *The Signature of God*, Rhonda Milner uses her talents and training to illustrate how God reveals Himself in His creation and our lives. Drawing on her medical background, she examines the intricate beauty of the workings of the human body but then also shares her observations as a young child from stories of nature handed down to her by her grandmother. She shows how God has made Himself known through her personal tragedies of loss to guide readers to a place of hope and blessing. If you are not a believer or question God's existence, you will be certain of His loving presence after reading this astute thesis. This is must-read, no matter your faith background."

—MARY JANE STAFFORD, Founder and Chief Executive Officer of Grateful Hearts Ministries

"Rhonda Milner touches us from a place of deep personal knowing of who the ultimate Source of life is. She reminds us that God's intelligence is present in every particle of creation and that in nature, we can discern the astounding depth of His love for us. All He asks is for us to tune in through constant mindfulness, prayer, and gratitude. In *The Signature of God*, Milner provides a primer on how to do it."

—TIMOTHY QUINNAN, PhD, author, screenwriter, and President of Richmont Graduate University

Also by Rhonda Dawes Milner

The Mended Heart: A Poet's Journey through
Love, Suffering, and Hope

The

Signature of
GOD

His Name Written into Our Lives & the World

Rhonda Dawes Milner, MD, MA, LPC

RIVER GROVE
B O O K S

Handwritten inscription:

To Beth,
May you
always feel God's
loving presence
surrounding you.
God bless you.
Dawes Milner
Romans 1:20

Published by River Grove Books
Austin, TX
www.rivergrovebooks.com

Distributed by River Grove Books

Design and composition by Greenleaf Book Group
Cover design by Greenleaf Book Group
Dogwood Tree Under Blue Sky by Marls Images. Used under license
from Shutterstock.com
Interior Images: ©Stefano Borsa; Tina Andros Ch123; Checubus; frank60; stephen reich; Triff;
Tsekhmister; koya979; Anton Khrupin; MJTH; aabeele; Kristopher Bell; Sergei Mironenko;
Rene Baars; Glass and Nature; Galyna Andrushko; Erik Unger; wacomka; Jelena Yukka;
Nickolai Repnitskii; nanoman; Szasz-Fabian Jozsef; inspirf; Billion Photos; NadyaEugene;
Ozerov Alexander; Mike Ver Sprill; Grodfoto. Used under license from Shutterstock.com

Publisher's Cataloging-in-Publication data is available.

Print ISBN: 978-1-63299-225-3

eBook ISBN: 978-1-63299-226-0

First Edition

*For my loved ones and all others, so
that they may know the depths of
God's love for them.*

Contents

Preface

THE CONCEPT OF THIS BOOK ORIGINATED SOME YEARS ago when I began to recollect stories that my grandmother had passed on to me when I was a little girl. These were stories from her own childhood that told of how different things in nature represented God's love for us in Jesus Christ. As an adult, this brought to my awareness the possibility that other signs in nature were waiting for me to notice and discover them.

I began to see the world differently, and things that had before been hidden became more beautiful and clear. I kept a running list of symbols, metaphors, and signs that I observed, and eventually, thinking that all the evidence of God's presence in nature might make a great discussion of apologetics with tangible evidence of God's existence, I suggested the topic to my spiritual mentor, Ken Boa. I told him that there were so many of these symbols around us—their patterns, existence, and beauty appearing in such intricacy and with such detail—that they could not possibly have happened by sheer coincidence or randomness; there was something bigger going on, and I could see that God was using it to tell us His own love story.

Ken listened to me talk that day and then recommended that I write this book. After giving it some thought, I decided to pursue the idea. I've aspired to make this into a book that a child, adolescent, college student, scientist, skeptic, atheist, or any curious, seeking person could relate to in some capacity.

The other reason you now have this book in your hands is connected to my journey of faith—my walk with Jesus. I was, as Christians say, "born again" on Easter Sunday of 1990, following the birth of my youngest daughter, who was three months premature. Though I attended church, I didn't know at the time that I didn't yet have a personal faith. I knew a lot about religion, and going to church was something I understood; but my heart did not know who Jesus really was.

On Easter Sunday that year, the minister at my church preached a sermon on the well-known premises of C. S. Lewis and Josh McDowell, two theologians from different times and contexts who shared a real and similar faith. Both these theologians reasoned that if we believe Jesus actually lived according to what history shows us, then it's important to figure out who He was and what He was about.[1] Either Jesus truly was the Son of God, as He claimed, or the way He lived his life indicated He was a liar or a lunatic. During this sermon, I realized that if Jesus was truly God's Son, and the only way to God, the Father, was through Jesus, then Jesus could not merely have been just a good, kind man or even a prophet; His claims were bigger than that. Either He was lying and crazy or He was who He said He was. I knew also that many of His followers throughout history had been martyred because they believed He was the Son of God; I couldn't imagine that someone would give up their life for something that was less than the truth.

That day, I realized what Christ had done for me personally, the sacrifice that He had made so that my sins could be cleansed. I accepted Him as my Savior, and from that point, I began my real walk in life with Jesus. I began to learn and discover who He is and who I am in Him. And I began to discern God's will for my life by what happened to me.

I joined a women's Bible study to learn about God, Jesus, and the

Holy Spirit through God's written Word, the Bible. I went to Ken Boa's Sunday School class and then his Bible studies. (As an Oxford scholar, my mentor approached the Bible with both an intellectual and a pragmatic approach that made a lot of sense and greatly appealed to me.) I also became interested to know what great theologians had to say about the Bible and began to study their thoughts on the Christian faith. At the time, I read the writings of people like John of the Cross, Teresa of Ávila, St. Augustine, Brother Lawrence, George MacDonald, Søren Kierkegaard, Viktor Frankl, C. S. Lewis, and Friedrich Bonhoeffer, as well as books by contemporary writers like Gary W. Moon, Larry Crabb, Siang-Yang Tan, Josh McDowell, Lee Strobel, Richard Foster, Dallas Willard, and Malcolm Muggeridge.

In addition, I took an interest in how God seemed present in science and the natural world. I read as much as I could by scientists who have faith, like Hugh Ross and Francis Collins, and also physicians, like Gerald May, Larry Dossey, and Bernie Siegel. In all of it, I discovered a common thread in the writings: that there is truth that stands outside of time, something bigger that I recognized and now understand as God's Eternal Truth. This realization helped me to become even more devoted to my faith and belief.

At the same time my faith was developing and I was beginning to look at the world around me differently, I was facing serious challenges in my personal life. My older daughter was struggling with a serious, life-threatening eating disorder, which led to a serious, life-threatening drug addiction. My older son was struggling with behavioral challenges in school because of learning disabilities and ADHD. All four of my children, in fact, had ADHD with learning disabilities. My children's struggles were heartbreaking and seemingly insurmountable, and as much as I tried to help them, I knew I was limited in my ability to make things better. Then, during this same time, my beloved mother was diagnosed with Alzheimer's disease.

I found, in the midst of all these trials, that my faith had become such a source of confidence, strength, and hope that I felt like I could prevail through my troubles. I grew to have a reliance on Jesus, understanding He was with me in the hardships every step of the way. And I began to turn more and more to friends who had a strong faith and who came alongside me with help, prayer, and support that seemed beyond the norm. It was like God working through them to show me He was there.

That was when a small group of us formed a prayer group of five. As friends, we bonded together not only because we shared our faith but also because we all had children who were going through challenges and troubles. I learned an interesting truth at that time that still holds true even now: God seems to get our attention as parents through our children. When our children hurt, we hurt; we listen in, we look for help, we come to the end of ourselves, we call out to God. And He shows us He's there. I understand now that God, in His amazing wisdom, brought a group of five women together during that time, letting us think that our need for one another was mostly about our children; but it was really about us and how He was working in our lives. Though we were able to better help and love our kids, we realized that we were growing in the process and that we were changing. This journey with my friends has continued through deep sorrows, devastating losses, incredible miracles, amazing love, and God's goodness and plan through it all.

Along the way, I became a runner because I found that it gave me an opportunity each day to enjoy a quiet time and be in prayer with God. It was while I was running and praying one day that my life shifted in a new direction. Even now, I remember where I was on my run—the exact street—the exact spot—when God spoke clearly to me in that still, quiet voice of His. I had been running and thinking about my life and the years to come. I had been reflecting on my role as a mother, my work as a physician, and my journey of faith. My youngest, a daughter, was thirteen years old at the time and entering high school; I realized that when she went off to college, I would have a life without my children being there every day. There was an end in sight to a phase of life that I loved and knew so well. I thought about who I was and what I was about in life. Then, I heard God's voice—an answer—in my mind. He said that in my role as a physician, I worked to heal the body, which is temporary and in the temporal realm; but I felt Him tell me that I was supposed to enlarge my view and use who I was to do what truly matters: become a doctor of the soul to heal souls for eternity. What difference did it make as a physician to heal one's temporal body if the soul was not healed for eternity?

I did not know it then, but these thoughts were Scripture from the Bible. Second Corinthians 4:18 states, "So we fix our eyes not on what is seen, but on what is unseen. For what is seen is temporary, but what is unseen is eternal." I believe that we all have many thoughts and can sometimes have a hard time distinguishing them from God's messages to us; in order for us to know that God is speaking to us, we need His words and direction to be based in Scripture. On this particular day, God brought to my mind a connection between my experience as a physician and my desire to help people in an eternal sense.

Some years later, a dear friend of mine from my small prayer group happened to tell me about a graduate school with a Christian spiritual focus that produced master's-level counselors trained in theology, psychology, and the integration of the two. Because we shared challenges with our children as teenagers, my friend recognized a need for this type of counselor. Knowing that we both would have wished for our children to be able to benefit from this kind of therapy, my friend mentioned the school to me with the idea that we should raise money to support its programs. She persuaded me to go tour the school with her to learn more about it.

I believe God engineered the circumstances of my life to take me on that tour and provide me with a plan for what He'd shown me on my run in years prior. The tour that day not only convinced me of my purpose in work but also paved the way to my future. I even remember meeting the president of the school at the time and saying to him, "This is where I am supposed to be as a student and where God wants me."

I came home from the campus tour and told my husband that I was returning to school to pursue a master's in professional counseling. He was shocked, needless to say, but he also knew me to be the kind of person who did not change her mind when she was determined to do something.

I applied for graduate school, not knowing logistically how to make it all work. But I believed that if I was being obedient to God and looked to Him for guidance and direction, He would make it happen and help me along the way. I also recognized that it's so easy to delay our plans when life and other obstacles get in the way; I didn't want to let the opportunity go by when I knew He had led me to that point. Fortunately, because I already had a medical degree and had completed postgraduate work, I met the requirements for admission. I watched, with gratefulness, as God opened the necessary doors for me, and I made sure to walk through them. In truth, I leaped through the doors with blind abandon!

So, I found myself starting graduate school at the age of fifty-four, a surprising turn of events, given that I was older, had raised four children, had changed careers, and hadn't even known a few months beforehand that this would be my plan. Interestingly enough, the university was only five minutes away from my neighborhood and was located behind the church I attended. I had never thought much about the university before then and, in fact, never paid attention to its existence. God has such a sense of humor, and I knew that because of the proximity, I would likely not ever miss a class in graduate school or a church service on a Sunday. He had made it as convenient as could be for me to answer His calling.

Today, I hold two master's degrees—one in professional counseling and one in ministry. During my studies, I specialized in the areas of addiction and spirituality. Today, I am a licensed professional counselor who treats clients who cannot afford regular counseling. I also hold certificates in spiritual direction and spiritual formation and am an ordained nondenominational minister.

As a microbiology major at the University of Georgia and a medical student at Emory University School of Medicine in my younger years, I never had to write papers. Mostly, I studied, worked hard, and took exams. But as a graduate student later in life, I suddenly found myself writing papers all the time. I think all that writing is what eventually gave me the confidence to write the book you now hold in your hands.

I believe God's presence is everywhere and simultaneously within us. He is with us every second of our lives. For every miraculous beat of our heart, every intake of breath, every thought we have, He is present. In every detail of the world, every blade of grass, every sunset, every breeze, He is present. Throughout this book, I seek to analyze the signature that God left for us to see. So many signs in creation reveal He exists and demonstrate His love for us. If we only look for His signature, we'll know He's there.

God's Signature

Since what may be known about God is plain to them, because God has made it plain to them. For since the creation of the world God's invisible qualities—his eternal power and divine nature—have been clearly seen, being understood from what has been made, so that people are without excuse.

ROMANS 1:19–20

WE LIVE IN A WORLD OF NATURAL WONDER, FILLED WITH beautiful and amazing marvels—roaring waterfalls, intricate rock formations, lush green forests, magnificent night skies. The fact that they exist says something. The intricacy in their details is astonishing. The way they work is awe-inspiring. And I believe the purpose they serve is nothing short of miraculous.

Whether in nature, physics, the biology of our own human bodies, or the situations of our lives, things are not as they are by accident. So much in the natural order points to a master plan—and, I would say, a master Creator. We live in a world where invisible electromagnetic waves allow us to use technology, the earth's atmosphere creates an ideal environment for us to live in, and gravity enables us to orbit around the sun. We are people who can think, feel, move, and function because of brain signals that travel to all the parts of our bodies at incredible speeds. We receive joy, peace, help, and inspiration through nature and all of God's creation.

You may, at times, have experienced the way the quietness of a garden, the vastness of a field, or the enormity of a mountain draws out certain emotions in you or gives you clarity of thought. I believe God uses nature and His Creation to have a relationship with us. He's designed things in amazing, intricate ways to show us He's there and He loves us.

Nature displays tremendous glory, creativity, and diversity of beauty. There isn't only one kind of tree; there are tens of thousands. And within one species of tree, each one is unique in its thickness, height, and shape. Each tree has its place in the world for a reason; and it grows to its full potential according to the water and nutrients available to it.

When we take a good look at nature and the way things work, I believe we come up against the question of how the beauty, detail, and majesty of it all is even possible. How can we not marvel at the natural world and the way we receive from and participate in it? To look means we're seeing something bigger than ourselves, something that happens regardless of us, and yet we are a part of it.

This leads me to the idea of a signature.

If God created the universe and our natural world, like any artist, He would have signed His name to His work of art so that those who view it and recognize its beauty and intricacy would know who the artist is. And not only did He sign His name to let us know He's the Creator, He also built evidence into His creation to give us a way to know Him, His nature, and His character. It stops me in my tracks to think of how, on top of creating the world and everything in it, He also uses nature and natural phenomena to communicate His love for us. Since we are created in His image, by knowing more about Him, we're able to know more about ourselves, our possibilities, and our potential.

If we look for, notice, and recognize the signs God leaves for us in His natural world, we have an opportunity to see into the mind of our Maker. I believe God wants us—His creation—to know that He desires to have a loving relationship with us; and when we come to understand the way He views us, we are moved to love Him back.

I also believe that when we take the time to look at our natural world with our eyes and hearts open, the things in life that may before have seemed mundane or simple are suddenly extraordinary and profound in the way they clarify the mystery of existence. When we look beyond the expected, we find the unexpected in a world of intricate design and beauty, full and overflowing with meaning and significance. We begin to sense and understand that *we* have significance and purpose and are a part of the magnificent glory of God.

God signs His name on more than nature. He signs it on all of creation. And that includes us.

A Signature Analysis

A person's signature is a conscious form of expression to communicate how he or she wants to be seen by others. Handwriting reveals the writer's intellect, self-image, natural abilities, integrity, hidden aptitudes, and social behavior. If all this is true, it stands to reason that God's signature would communicate something about who He is and what His character is.

The thirteen chapters in this book describe aspects about God that I believe He wants us to know when we look at and observe the natural world and our lives. They highlight:

1. His simplicity and wonder

2. His existence and constancy

3. His intelligence and genius

4. His power and strength

5. His comfort and presence

6. His glory and majesty

7. His miracles and creativity

8. His mystery and omniscience

9. His truth and wisdom

10. His love and acceptance

11. His grace and mercy

12. His blessings and affirmations

13. His joy and hope

God's signature is evident in the world all around us, and His qualities are found in His creation. His signature is personal and stylized; it says something important about how He wants us to perceive Him. We can study the way He signs His name as any handwriting analyst might—by looking closely at size, placement, direction, slant, content, legibility, or strokes. And as we do, we come to see that He's signed His name in a way that no one else possibly can.

Why the Natural World?

The Bible shows us that Jesus was fond of parables, allegories, metaphors, and symbols with hidden meanings. It seems that God, as Jesus's Father and also His likeness, would also likely do the same thing, using His creation to reveal hidden meaning and knowledge about Him for people to discover.

In the Old Testament, countless symbols and signs point readers to the New Testament, representing Christ and His love and sacrifice for us. The tabernacle of the Old Testament, for example, is made significant in the New Testament when Jesus becomes the real tabernacle for all people. The blood that had to be shed by sacrificial animals in Old Testament times is understood as powerful and meaningful when Christ later sheds His own blood and allows Himself to be sacrificed on the Cross in order to atone for our sins. And the shepherds of the Old Testament who did the hard and humble work of tending to flocks are viewed differently when Christ, in the New Testament, identifies Himself as the shepherd who loves and cares for His flock: all of us. I believe a God who would leave us signs and symbols throughout history and in His Bible would likely also do this for us in nature and His creation. God, being who He is, would probably have conceived of and designed the natural world and the science of everything from the beginning of time in order to always give us a way to know Him.

Since God loves every single one of us and does not want to lose anyone, He would design a way to connect with us, provide for us, and show us He cares. Even a person who lives in a remote or hard-to-reach part of the world, without the benefits of the Bible and the Gospel, would be able to, on some level, acknowledge there's something bigger or more miraculous at play. In the book *I'm Glad You Asked*, Ken Boa, president of Reflections Ministries and Trinity House Publishers, and Larry Moody, president of Search Ministries, write, "The creation points beyond itself to the One who made it, and no one can plead ignorance of the Creator, because all people have access to this general revelation of God."[1] The Bible and the Gospel are God's overt ways of showing His presence and love, but nature can reveal Him, too. God wants to be sure that we have every opportunity to know Him and to spend eternity with our Beloved Father and Christ.

Reading God's Signature

This book is founded on the premise that nature, the universe, and God's interaction with us through His creation reveal a whole lot about Him and how He feels about us. What you'll read in these pages barely begins to even scratch the surface of who He is and all that He's made. But I think you'll find that God is beautiful, amazing, and creative—and so good to demonstrate Himself to us in the countless ways He does.

My hope is that as you think about and consider my own thoughts, reflections, and studies on all this, you'll come to know Him more. The writing of this book—and honestly, my whole Christian journey—is not just a process of intellectual knowledge or cognitive understanding. It's an act of faith led by God's Holy Spirit, a moment-by-moment decision to trust, an experience of wonder and hope. As you seek Him through the words on these pages and in the world around you, I pray you find Him.

Part 1

God's Signature in Creation

CHAPTER 1

God's Simplicity and Wonder

And He said: "Truly I tell you, unless you change and become like little children, you will never enter the kingdom of heaven."

MATTHEW 18:3

GOD TELLS US WHO HE IS IN COUNTLESS WAYS. SOMETIMES He chooses to do this through small, simple wonders in the natural world, objects we may have seen hundreds of times before but overlooked. Other times, He grabs our attention in bigger ways, and we may wonder how we haven't noticed Him there all along. I believe God has always revealed His love for us in the beauty and seeming simplicity of nature and that these things communicate significant truths about His character.

I also believe God delights in revealing Himself for us. It's like offering us encouragement and glimpses of His glory through nature. These signs of Him help us to persevere, to think about who we are in the big scheme of things, and to realize there's something bigger and better at play. And He does this for all of us. Any one of us can see, observe, and enjoy the traces and glimpses of Him in nature.

As a little girl, I listened to my grandmother tell me stories about God's creation, stories that pointed directly to Him and particularly to Christ and the significance of the Cross. These stories opened my eyes, and I began to look at the natural world differently, seeing Him everywhere. To this day, I continue to be amazed that God created the natural order in a way that provokes such a sense of wonder and awe.

When we look at nature, I think it's important to see it as if from a child's perspective. Marvel in it. Take joy in it. Revel in its amazing simplicity and the powerful message it sends about who God is. We tend to become bogged down as adults, to overthink, to become distracted. In this chapter, I'll share with you some of the observations my grandmother made and a few of the wonders we can receive when we view nature through a simpler, more childlike lens.

My hope is that you'll see Him not only in the details I describe in this chapter but also in the nature He's chosen to place around you.

The Simplicity and Wonder of Trees

Occasionally, you may notice something particular about a tree—its size, the curve of a branch, the color of its leaves, the texture of its bark. But while we appreciate trees, it's also easy to gloss over them much of the time. How often do you walk past a tree, knowing that it's there but not truly seeing it or thinking much about it? If we were to stop for a moment to regard the tree differently, to appreciate it and to contemplate its value, we might gain some interesting insights.

Human civilization is dependent upon trees, not only because trees offer us important resources but also because they provide us with ecological benefits. We know they produce oxygen and clean the air, for example. They also regulate precipitation, offer a natural defense against flooding, provide habitats for animals, cool the earth, and prevent soil erosion.

Trees, when you really think about it, are wondrous.

Have you ever stood next to a California coastal redwood tree? Redwoods are the tallest trees in the world. They can grow to around 350 feet high, and in some cases, if you were to stand at the bottom of one of these trees, you wouldn't be able to see its top. They've also been known to live up to around two thousand years old, which means it was possible for them to have existed when Jesus Himself walked the earth. Standing next to one of these glorious, ancient, and slightly intimidating trees, you might feel insignificant in size and humbled to realize the span of your life on earth in relation to them.

This tree also provides some of the strongest, most durable wood in the world. People often select furniture or construction materials made of redwood because they know it will last and not decay like other woods. It's resistant to warping, rotting, and even termites. And it's known for its beauty and color.

The redwood tree is a magnificent symbol of God's own glory and magnificence. It is not only larger, grander, stronger, and more enduring than we are, but also completely breathtaking to behold. I believe God uses the redwood to point us to Him.

Though I could go into the details and particulars of other tree species, I want to address another aspect of appreciating God's natural wonder. Every tree is a miracle in and of itself. Even smaller trees display God's glory. But you don't necessarily have to understand the science or be an expert on trees in order to know that what you're seeing is wondrous. (You can witness a bolt of lightning, for example, and be amazed by it, but at the same time be unable to comprehend how and why it happened.) Simply accepting nature at face value will also allow you to receive it. This would be similar to the way a child might notice, be curious about, and marvel at something in nature. It doesn't have to be complicated.

A few years ago, I received an email sometime before Easter—one of those emails that people forward to each other. In this email, I noticed a photo that featured what appeared to be hundreds of pine trees, each of them sprouting with new growth. The tops of the pine trees in the photo appeared as hundreds of crosses, and I remember the absolute astonishment I felt when I realized that pine trees really do that. It was as if the pine trees themselves were giving glory to Christ and pointing to the Cross. I know I had my mind on Easter, but I also believe that observations like this are not coincidences; they are often God speaking to our hearts. When we look at nature (even in a photo sent through an email), we can see His presence, and it might be a breathtaking, moving, and emotional experience because we sense it is God demonstrating His love for us. He reaches out to us and lifts us up to Him, even in simple, unassuming ways. But the simplicity doesn't negate the profundity of the experience.

We can also view trees as symbols. My grandmother used to talk to me about the dogwood tree, which, in the South where I grew up, blooms around Easter. Though I knew the story she told me about this tree was a legend, I felt that it still said something about what Jesus went through for us when He was punished and crucified. According to the legend, the dogwood tree was, a long time ago in Israel, prized as one of the finest, noblest, and most impressive of trees. It grew straight and tall, and its wood was good and strong. Legend has it that the dogwood was selected as the tree that would be used as the wood for Jesus's cross, and it felt great sadness for the role it played in His crucifixion. The story goes on to say that Jesus sensed this and, in His compassion, altered the nature of the tree so that rather than being tall and stately, future dogwoods would be small and thin; then, in this way, it would never need be used for a crucifixion again. The dogwood today is a small-sized tree with beautiful blossoms and distinctive branching. Though I know the story my grandmother told me was just a story, I love the way the dogwood blooms every Easter as a meaningful reminder of Christ's love for us. The tree seems to be blooming in celebration of Jesus's resurrection.

The Simplicity and Wonder of Flowers

The dogwood tree is also fascinating to me because of its blooms. People love to admire this gorgeous tree in the springtime, and regardless of their religious background, they observe the same physical characteristics that I do in the flowers of the dogwood. My grandmother showed me how the dogwood blossom has four large petals that are, interestingly enough, shaped like a cross. Its petals are often white, which she said signifies Christ's white robes of purity. (Sometimes the petals are pink, which, in keeping with the legend, symbolizes that the tree is blushing in shame for the role it played in Jesus's crucifixion.) The edge of each petal is notched at its tip, representing Christ's wounds, and each of these notches has a red tinge, representing Christ's blood. In the center of the blossom is a crown-like cluster, which represents Christ's crown of thorns. And as the flower ages, it appears speckled, some say with blood-like spatters.

Though people may assert that these connections are unrelated, there is something interesting and uncanny about them. We will, of course, always see things from our own worldview; but I believe there's something to be said for even loose associations between things. They require us to be open minded, to consider possibilities, and to think objectively about the relationships between ideas. If we look with the eyes of a child, we might see something surprising and new.

When I find myself in nature, I also can't help but to connect what I see on an emotional level to bigger themes in life and, in particular, to God. Have you ever been hiking and all of a sudden stumbled upon a field of beautiful wildflowers? There they are, in the middle of nowhere, not having been planted by man, but God. It's as if they are quietly and patiently waiting to be discovered, though even if you had not found them, they would still be there, present in all their beauty and glory. I'm always struck by the fact that they are like a gift to us, if only we can find them. And then I'm reminded about how in the Bible Jesus says He's waiting patiently at the door to be discovered by us.

In Revelation 3:20, He tells us, "Here I am! I stand at the door and knock. If anyone hears my voice and opens the door, I will come in and eat with that person, and they with me." Like the field of wildflowers that's waiting for us to find it, Jesus is there, waiting for us to find Him. Like the field of wildflowers is full of beauty and offers us a sense of joy and awe, Jesus is full of beauty and offers us His joy, love, peace, and help. Like the field of wildflowers is a gift that God gives to us, Jesus is the ultimate gift that God wants to share with us.

Let's also look at what a rose might say about God. In North American culture, we often give roses to our sweethearts and those we love because roses symbolize love. They are beautiful flowers with a lot of meaning attached. When we offer roses to someone, they typically no longer have the thorns that are present when they're first picked. These thorns can hurt, like love can hurt when someone takes a risk or makes themselves vulnerable. But unless we're willing to open ourselves up to love, we'll never be able to fully appreciate and experience the beautiful gift it is and the richness it brings to our life. Jesus willingly made Himself vulnerable for us, opening Himself up to rejection, condemnation, pain, and suffering in order to bring us the real, enduring love He knows we need. He accepted that to bring us great love, He would need to open Himself up to pain and to sacrifice Himself for us. Jesus is not unlike a magnificent rose when He is described in historical accounts as wearing a crown of thorns on His head. The beauty of the rose and the beauty of Jesus are not all they seem to be. I believe we are able to enjoy and receive them because there's an aspect of pain to them—and this came at a cost. To pluck the beautiful rose, blood may be drawn from the sharp, piercing thorns. For us to have a beautiful, eternal life, the price was the blood of Jesus.

Similarly, we're not able to have love in our hearts unless someone gives it to us. At the end of my high school career, the quote I chose to feature underneath my graduation picture in the yearbook was, "Love was not put in your heart to stay. Love is not love until you give it away." It was a simple but profound concept to ponder at the time and continues to ring true for me today. It's made even more significant as I contemplate God on my faith journey and consider how He speaks to us so powerfully and so beautifully through the objects in His creation. I find that it serves to set my focus for how to live life as well. When I see a rose, I can remember that it is in the giving of love that love comes to be. Only then can it do what it needs to do in our hearts and lives. Jesus is love in action, and His name is not only synonymous with love, but He is love itself.

Nature, with all of its metaphors, is so full of God's love for us. When we become aware of and see all the symbols surrounding us, we can connect the dots and find that they lead to one place: They point to Jesus and the Father.

The Simplicity and Wonder of Seasons

It's a miracle that seasons exist. God created them to serve a purpose on earth, and without them, scientists say we would be in a sorry state. We recognize seasons as a revolving cycle of life and death, predictable to us and often familiar in their characteristics. Yet seasons have wondrous and profound implications, which say important things about God.

Deciduous trees, for example, lose their leaves in the fall. The leaves simply fall off because they have died and no longer need to be attached to their source of life. The same trees in the wintertime are devoid of foliage—as if dead themselves. But in the spring, with warmth and rain, a miracle happens. The trees bud with new life and the fresh, pale green of growth from seemingly nothing. Death begets new life, a new beginning, and before long, the tree looks vibrant and alive, with new leaves budding off the same limbs that the dead leaves had been attached to. Does this not mirror our own life's journey, both in a physical and spiritual sense?

In the physical sense, springtime represents our birth as a fresh, new bud. We grow into maturity, as a tree does in the summer. We begin to fade in the autumn. We die (or appear as dead) in the winter.

In the spiritual sense, we are born into the world. We grow, learn, and explore life, its meaning, and its purpose. We come to recognize that Christ is our savior, knowing that something big in us must change in order to live out what we now know is true. Christians refer to this as a "dying" of the old self. Though no one is technically dying, it's a spiritual dying that signifies the changing of a life and a natural shift in the way we might think about things. A fall leaf, as it dies (to its old self), can be perceived as producing a colorful display of beauty, not unlike the display of beauty that might happen with our change of heart with belief. Then the leaf dies and is released from its old life, not unlike the death of our old self. But springtime comes, and our identity in Christ is like new, and we are born again as little budding Christians that must grow into a more mature state as we take up our spiritual pilgrimage.

So what's in a falling leaf or in the budding of a new one? I think God uses these to show us that even though we die to our old way of being, in Jesus can be a new life that will come. He loves all of us, old and new, but uses leaves—and, indeed, the seasons—to remind us of His hope and love. The seasons are part of His great plan to save us.

I find it fascinating that Easter is in the springtime. When I think of spring, I picture the dormant seed sprouting with new life, trees blossoming and bearing leaves and fruit, flowers pushing up through the ground, baby animals newly born, birds making their nests and laying eggs, hatching new lives of baby birds. To me, countless signs in nature in the springtime show rebirth and new beginnings. I'm someone who doesn't believe in coincidences, so I can't help but be reminded of the resurrection of Christ in the spring. It seems more than fitting to me that Easter is in the spring. I believe all we need to do is look with childlike openness in order to see a world that speaks God's name and displays His glorious wonder.

In 2011 my oldest son died suddenly in an accident. The funeral program was especially important to me, as it was an opportunity to bear witness to my son's and my faith. For the memorial service, I wrote about the magic of a seed, using it as a metaphor for my son's growth and passage to Heaven. The seed, in the darkness of the ground, begins to germinate from within, growing from the spring rains that nurture it. At the chosen moment, it breaks forth from its shell and, as it outgrows its dark world, the little flower bursts from the soil to find its new world of bright sunlight. The seed is discarded, giving forth to a new life. In the same way, the little flower, my beautiful son, outgrew his earthly body and left the darkness to be in the light—to be in the presence of the Lord, to be in Heaven.

The seasons in a year aren't the only ideas that signify death and resurrection. Jonathan Edwards, the famous eighteenth-century American revivalist preacher, philosopher, and theologian, recognized that God also built this symbolism into the hours in a day. He noted that every night, death is represented in the act of going to sleep, and in the morning, resurrection is represented in our process of waking up. Each day, we are born again, fresh and new, with all the possibilities for a day before us and the opportunity to start again. In God, we have the hope of fresh beginnings, and the morning is always to come. I love that God has created the natural order in our world in these profoundly simple ways. If we look for them, we can find them. And when we see them, we see Him.

I believe God not only designed seasons for a reason but also within them created amazing and wondrous elements. As with all of nature's metaphors, they give us a picture of who God is and how He loves us. As a little girl, I was always fascinated with snowflakes. How was it possible that every single snowflake, just a tiny frozen crystal of water, could look so unique and like no other snowflake? Even if two snowflakes were to be formed in the same area, their journeys to the ground would be different, impacting their size and shape. How they form is reflected by the way water molecules arrange themselves and by the temperature during crystallization. Though scientists have now determined that most snowflakes fall into one of thirty-some different shapes, the stunning diversity of snowflakes and the detailed structures of their crystals remains a marvel. They remind me that we are, in many ways, like these little snowflakes, each of us unique, special, and beautiful the way God created us. We are formed in different ways, come from different places, and have different journeys. No two of us are alike, and yet God sees us all. He knows how we're made, what we've gone through, and where He'll choose to have us land.

On an even more basic level, snowflakes are simply beautiful and can evoke in us a sense of wonder. Have you ever seen, on a sunny winter day, the way snowflakes glisten as they fall from the sky? They sparkle like little prisms when the sunlight catches them at the right angle. It's a stunning sight, like diamonds sparkling as the snow falls to the ground. Beautiful details in God's creation, particularly ones that catch us off guard, convey a deep sense of gratefulness and wonder. We realize we get to witness something bigger than ourselves, something we, as human beings, could not create. And we recognize that these are gifts that sometimes last for only a few moments, reminders of God's love.

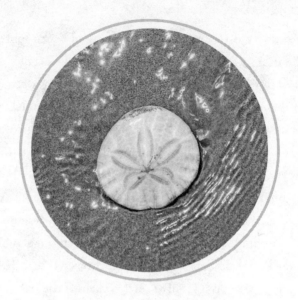

The Simplicity and Wonder of the Sea

I loved going to the ocean as a little girl, taking walks on the beach and collecting seashells. My grandmother knew this and used to tell me the beautiful story of the sand dollar, a flat, circular sea urchin that lives in the sea. People say that the sand dollar depicts the birth and death of Jesus Christ in several ways:

- Its roundness has been likened to the roundness of the world, which Jesus was born into and came to save.

- On the top, flat side of the sand dollar looks to be a star, which is said to represent the Star of Bethlehem, the phenomenon in the sky that alerted the Magi that Jesus had been born.

- The star sits in the center of an imprint of what looks like an Easter lily, signifying the death or crucifixion of Christ but also His resurrection.

- And also on this side of the sand dollar, you can spot five holes that look like piercings; four of the holes represent the nail holes used to hold Jesus to the Cross, and the fifth represents the spear that the Centurion guard used to pierce His abdomen.

- On the other side of the sand dollar, the texture appears as an imprint of a Christmas poinsettia, which again signifies Christ's birth.

- The sand dollar, when bleached from the sun, becomes white in color, symbolizing Christ's purity.

- If you crack the sand dollar open, you can find tiny pieces of its endoskeleton, each one uncannily shaped like a white dove. The white dove is a symbol of God's Holy Spirit, who was sent by God to help us and give us hope and comfort; it also represents Christ and His resurrection.

- Had the sea urchin not died, we would not be able to appreciate the sand dollar in the same way. Similarly, if not for Jesus's death, we would not be able to appreciate and receive the gift of life He gives us through His sacrifice and resurrection.

It's amazing to me that this little humble creature of the sea has been given God's glory in order to represent the story of His Son and to tell of when Jesus came to earth to save humankind and give us salvation. Even in its death, it encourages us in life. Could it be a coincidence that all these characteristics are there? Some might say so. But could it also be possible that God, as the Creator and artist of all things, made these details because He is who He is? Take another look at the sand dollar and consider how, when viewed through a different lens, it might be an example of God's signature in the world. The work of an artist is determined by who they are; their sensibilities and inspirations can be found in the work itself.

When I walk along beaches, I also pick up seashells. As a child, I was always amazed at how I could pick up a shell, put it to my ear, and hear the noise of the ocean. I thought about how the ocean was where the shell had come from; its origin was the ocean. To me, this was another way that God chose to have His creation point to its origin, to Him.

I remember also once coming across a larger shell, tangled within some seaweed. As I stooped to pick the shell up, I noticed hundreds of perfect little micro-shells, each only a millimeter or two wide but almost an exact replica of a larger shell. The existence of the tiny shells drew my attention to the larger shell because I considered them in relation to one another. The larger shell was my frame of reference. In much the same way, people who believe in Jesus are image-bearers of Christ, meaning their existence points to Him. And Jesus, by the sheer fact that He exists and is who He says He is, causes our focus to go to *His* origin, God, the Creator.

The ocean, like God, is vast and powerful with marvelous mysteries and so many organisms unknown beneath its surface. It is full of amazing life. I believe God created oceans to serve a specific purpose on our planet and in our lives. It produces more than half of the world's oxygen, it regulates our climate and weather patterns, and it provides food, medicine, and other resources. Even if you live far inland, nowhere near the ocean, it still affects your life. The air you breathe, food you eat, water you drink, and products you use can come from—or be brought to you by—the ocean. I believe it demonstrates God's magnificence and creativity. It is a wonder and a gift, intricate in design and with His name all over it.

Where We Fit in the Big Scheme of Things

When I was young, I had an ant farm, as many kids did. I was always fascinated when I studied the tunnels that the ants formed and observed the organization of their little communities, a microcosm of ours. I imagined the way God might view us from His vantage point, observing the way we bustle around, build things, join or leave communities. The ants I watched seemed oblivious to me, and I doubted they had much of a clue or real knowledge of the big picture of life. Did they know who I was or that I was watching them? Did they know that I had a certain kind of power because of my size and perspective? Did they know how many of them there were, each one focused on its present task, scurrying past others? As people, are we not a little bit of the same? And yet God, being God, cares about each and every one of us. He sees what we're doing from start to finish: He knows what we've accomplished, He's with us in our efforts, and He can tell where we're headed.

But He can see more: our worries, our thoughts, our problems. He knows better approaches and where we fit in the big scheme of things because He not only created the world and us, but He also knows how our story ends.

Why are we each so unique, and why do we matter? What is the purpose of everything? I think how we fit into the world is significant. If we believe God signed His name on all the miraculous things He created, wouldn't we, as His creation, also have His signature on us? He's made us for a reason, chosen to have us born in the moment of history and in the situation of life we're in, and created us in a meaningful and unique way. In a sense, we're a much-needed part of a gigantic jigsaw puzzle. Each of us could be likened to a tiny piece of the puzzle, unique in shape and design and meant to impact and contribute to the part of the puzzle where we're to be placed. If we were not in our unique spot, fitting together with and connecting to the other pieces, the puzzle could not be complete and the picture would have a hole in it. We have a place in the world that affects the natural order of things. We may not always be able to see the big picture that we're a part of, but I hope we look for how we fit and know that we're needed. God sees the entire picture and the grand scheme of things. He sees you, and you matter to Him.

As I contemplate ants, the natural world, and who we are in life, I'm grateful for the way He's created everything. Remember that God has signed His name on you and in nature in order to remind you that you are special and much loved. Take time to look around at what God has signed; view nature through different eyes. God is an intricate God who shows you His glory in simple and wondrous ways. He's created nature for all of us. Any one of us can see, observe, and enjoy it, whether we know Him or not. I believe the evidence is there—whether through a tree, a flower, a snowflake, or a seashell—and it points to a marvelous Creator.

God of Wonder

God of wonder, a child's pure delight
You are all around surrounding our sight

You are there for everyone to see
You make it simple, easy to believe

Little children run to Your bright beacon of light
They see all Your power and all Your might

Tiny babes are always protected and safe
All their pure souls are Yours to finally take

Built-in stories and metaphors are Your design
Plain, uncomplicated to understand and find

Little ones You love to watch dance and play
They hear Your words, know what You say

Your love is always there to shine
Having displayed Your character into
Your intricate design

Dark nights full of hopes on twinkling bright stars
Where You hold our magical dreams both near and far

You know our every desire and all our wishes
You hear our heartfelt prayers and give us secret
butterfly kisses

All of this is part of Your mammoth
eternal scheme and plan
Our faith and trust remain forever held
in Your loving hands

—Rhonda Dawes Milner

CHAPTER 2

God's Existence and Constancy

The heavens declare the glory of God; the skies proclaim the work of his hands. Day after day they pour forth speech; night after night they reveal knowledge. They have no speech, they use no words; no sound is heard from them. Yet their voice goes out into all the earth, their words to the ends of the world.

PSALM 19:1–4

OUR UNIVERSE WAS FORMED IN AN AMAZING WAY. THE fact that it works as it does shows the existence of a God who has always been here. His constant presence is seen everywhere we look in the natural world and is even supported by different fields of science. You may be surprised to discover that science itself can give testimony to God's existence and that there is a movement in the scientific community toward faith in God as Creator. In this chapter, I'll explore with you some ideas about science and our universe, so you can see that the world did not just happen by accident. As I do this, I hope you'll be encouraged to find that God is real, He is here, He is constant and dependable, and His character does not change.

The Big Bang Theory

The Bible says that the heavens and all of creation—in other words, the entire universe—by virtue of being how they are, prove that God made them. Genesis 1:1 says, "In the beginning God created the heavens and the earth." Psalm 19:1 says, "The heavens declare the glory of God," and "the skies proclaim the work of his hands." I believe God's signature can be found not only on the things He created but also in the way He created them.

Ideas surrounding the creation of the world have always created points of contention between people of different religious or scientific backgrounds. I'm fascinated by the fact that the big bang (also known as the origin of the universe) theory of creation is congruent with what the Bible says about creation.

About the Big Bang

Are you familiar with the big bang theory? It was first proposed in 1927 by Georges Lemaître, an astronomer and physics professor who suggested that the universe started as a single point, then expanded and stretched from that point to grow to the size it is. Not long afterward, astronomer Edwin Hubble observed that other galaxies were moving farther away from our galaxy and that the farthest galaxies seemed to be doing this faster than the closer ones. This suggested that the universe is still expanding. And if things were still moving farther apart, it also indicated that heavenly bodies, at some point in time, had started out closer together. Presumably the galaxies were still moving apart because of an explosion.

Physicist George Gamow lent important theoretical support to the big bang theory in the 1940s, posing that the universe had expanded from a single original cataclysm, somewhat like a nuclear bomb.[1] In 1964, scientists Arno Penzias and Robert W. Wilson discovered an annoying background noise coming from space, something later referred to as cosmic background radiation.[2] This is significant because the noise has been recognized as being secondary to the aftermath of the big bang from billions of years ago. The Hubble Ultra Deep Field telescope shows the state of the universe as it was some thirteen billion years ago. Scientists have also been able to see so far out into space that they've observed what amounts to one-trillionth of a second after the big bang, or all but .003 percent of the entire history of the universe.[3] Because of the way the speed of light works, scientists have been able to determine that the light detected by the Hubble telescope is light that comes from directly after the big bang, which essentially means that we are able to see back in time to right after the beginning of the universe. Again, this supports the idea that as we look farther out into space, the particles are farther apart because our universe is expanding from the central creation point of the big bang. All these findings confirm that there was a beginning to our universe, and there will be an end. Time will end after the expansion of the universe ends, when it will collapse on itself.

What's more, quantum physics has also recognized that there is no infinity to matter and that it is not possible to have infinitely small measurements.[4] This means that number measurements are not infinite in either direction, that there is a definable maximum and minimum quantifiable amount. Mathematicians also observed certain mysterious relationships of the various constants or factors.[5] These values of the constants in the forces binding certain particles appeared to be related mathematically to the number of the exact age of the universe. How strange is this coincidence? I believe it was part of an intricate plan to allow our human existence because our Creator desired it and designed it.

Quantum physics presents some other interesting data as well. The double-slit experiment of physics has shown that for light waves to convert into photons or particles, there must be a meaningful measurement;[6] but physicist Nick Herbert and others go on to show that it requires a conscious observer, the knowing in one's mind.[7] Quantum theory disclaims materialism in that consciousness precedes matter, according to Max Planck, one of the founders of quantum physics.[8] For a person of faith, this indicates that a greater consciousness of non-matter, timeless and spaceless, existed in the beginning or even prior to the beginning of creation. For me, this points to God, our Creator and Origin of all consciousness. It also means that our consciousness or soul will live on in the spiritual realm, pointing to an afterlife and what Scripture tells us happens after death.

The Need for a Creator

Something cannot come from nothing. Inorganic matter cannot beget organic matter. A rock cannot transform into human life or any other form of life. Everything has to have *some* origin and a way to begin. Many people offer compelling ideas about the origin of the universe, but every single one, including the big bang theory, points to the fact that a creator is necessary.

Physicist Albert Einstein's theory of relativity established that energy cannot be created or destroyed, only transformed. He showed us through his formula $E = mc^2$ that energy and matter are interchangeable, or in other words, different forms of the same thing. Energy can be converted to matter, and matter converted to energy. But if energy cannot be created or destroyed, where did the original energy come from that created the big bang? It could not have come from nothingness, because it would have lacked mass and energy. *Something* had to be able to create the energy. I've found, the more I've read and studied, that these scientific concepts all point to the idea of God as the Creator of the universe.

Even if you don't want to believe it—even if you prefer to think, for example, that we come from alien beings in another galaxy—it all still points to the need for a creator. Something cannot come from nothing. Someone had to be there at the beginning. Someone had to be able to make all of this.

According to the second law of thermodynamics of entropy, if matter is not interfered with in its natural state, the tendency is toward disorder to a lower energy state. (For example, if I didn't put effort into cleaning my house or washing dishes, it would turn into a mess or state of disorderliness.) Also, data from the Hubble Telescope has confirmed that space is expanding. This means that particles are moving apart as a result of the big bang, with energy gradually being lost by this slowing process of expansion. These concepts continue to point to the need for a creator. They point to God. Again, something (or someone) had to give the initial energy that caused the particles to come together against their natural state, since they would tend to spread apart. So they came together in great force, colliding and then exploding, to create the universe and life.

Scientists often try to find other explanations for the origin of the universe and the beginning of life. Physicist and cosmologist Stephen Hawking, for example, theorized that the big bang came from a black hole. But if this is true, who or what first created the black hole? Dr. Hawking was one of the most brilliant minds of our time, but his theory still ultimately led to the idea of a creator.

He also taught that the laws of relativity and laws of quantum mechanics could not exist together at the beginning of the universe; in other words, they oppose each other and could not have coexisted at the big bang. He stated that scientists had come up with a concept called "string theory" to explain the discrepancy of the coexistence of the two laws of nature. According to string theory, at least ten dimensions plus time existed at the time of creation, and then these folded in on themselves at the time of the big bang.[9] This would mean that other dimensions do or did exist. Similarly, Einstein thought there were four dimensions. Over time, he and other scientists have come up with many different theories about the universe and our natural world. When we encounter phenomena that seem unexplainable, why do we not look to God, who has signed His name on all of creation, for the answers? The fact that He exists can, in and of itself, offer explanations for some of the inconsistencies that have been observed in nature's fundamental laws. I continue to find, again and again, that any scientific attempts to explain the beginning of the universe still bring me back to the idea that, in order for something to exist, it must have a cause. Science provides us with a reason to trust that God exists and created the universe.

The Bible says in Psalm 148:3–5, "Praise him, sun and moon; praise him, all you shining stars. Praise him, you highest heavens and you waters above the skies. Let them praise the name of the Lord, for at his command they were created." Isaiah 40:26, 28 reads, "Lift up your eyes and look to the heavens: Who created all these? He who brings out the starry host one by one and calls forth each of them by name. Because of his great power and might strength, not one of them is missing. Do you not know? Have you not heard? The Lord is the everlasting God, the Creator of the ends of the earth." God has been there all along. The fact that our universe exists highlights the fact that *He* exists.

The Unexplainable

Believing some things in life and in our natural world requires a willingness to look at the facts of what God has laid out, but it also requires a degree of faith. On the surface this may sound unsatisfying to those who search for logical answers to their questions, especially in a scientific sense. But I believe God, as the one who created the universe and all of us, encourages our questions. He is not about us having a blind faith. In fact, He's big enough, wise enough, capable enough, and good enough to lead us to the answers. And He designed us to ask the tough questions and to think about things critically. In the Bible, Luke 10:27 says, "Love the Lord your God with all your heart and with all your soul and with all your strength and with all your *mind*" (emphasis added). How much greater would our worship of Him be if we sought Him and found Him on not just an emotional level but also an intellectual one? And wouldn't this better enable us to love Him with everything we've got? *That's* the kind of love and worship God wants from us. So don't be afraid to question and think. He can take it.

What's more, so many things exist in our natural world that we cannot see or hear, except through extraordinary means. Nonetheless, they are there. The fact that we can't see or hear them doesn't make them any less real. Many colors exist in the light spectrum, for example, that we cannot easily perceive; yet we benefit from infrared and ultraviolet light every day. Many sounds exist that we cannot perceive with the human ear; yet ultrasonic and infrasonic noises sound constantly in the world around us. We use powerful electron microscopes to detect tiny microbes, cells, and structures within cells, and we can also even use microscopes to view atoms. But we cannot view electrons or protons, so does that mean they don't exist? Of course not. Our inability to see or hear something does not mean we can't know something of its properties. In fact, sight and sound alone might, in certain cases, be too rudimentary an approach for some very real things out there.

How amazing that God would choose to love us and show us who He is through the creation of the world and His natural wonder. Some of His creation is more discernible to us. Some of it is still a mystery. We are, as humans, pretty intelligent; but we're not God, we weren't there at the beginning of time, and we have limitations to our understanding. The fact that we can't see and explain every aspect of what He's created doesn't mean the thing doesn't exist. We may be unable to detect something or observe all its qualities—but again, this doesn't mean it's not real.

Faith is much the same way. Simply because we can't easily observe something doesn't mean we have to be skeptical of it. We can think deeply about it, we can ask tough questions about it, and we can look into it. We're used to understanding things in the world in a certain way, but faith—in anything—calls us to be willing to believe something without seeing it, while at the same time, our heart, mind, and soul (some might even say gut) respond in agreement. You can have faith in someone you know, believing they'll accomplish something or deliver on a promise. Ultimately, faith in God is something like that, only with someone who is infallible, all-knowing, and utterly devoted to you. And He's like that whether you believe in Him or not.

Why do we so readily believe in other things we cannot see or hear, but not God?

A Divine Plan

Besides the big bang theory, scientists have also identified precise constants or values in physics that cannot be chalked up to coincidence.

They've determined that if these values were off by even a fraction, life could not exist. The precision in value of gravity and the electromagnetic fields, for example, are what permit life to exist; and if the values were less exact in any way, the world would not be. In other words, this is the idea that God made the earth precisely right for life, creating the exact conditions necessary for our survival.

Another principle talks about how humanity holds a special place in the universe. Brandon Carter, well-known astrophysicist and cosmologist from Cambridge University, presented something called the anthropic principle of the universe in 1973.[10] First noted by physicists Robert Dicke and John Wheeler, this principle recognizes that people are able to be observers of the universe's laws, recognizing their existence, because the laws are as they are in order to necessitate humankind's existence and capacity for observing them.[11] Put a little more simply, our ability to make any scientific observations about the universe is dependent on the fact that He exists. This is sort of like the chicken-or-the-egg concept. Which of these existences came first? The many unrelated fundamental constants in physics appear to have one thing in common: Their precise values were devised to specifically allow for our presence in the universe.

It's amazing to consider the idea that we are, it seems, the reason the universe exists; the universe exists for us to be able to have life. The constants and values, noted even by scientists, have been exactly construed to balance the existence of life as we know it. Our vast 13.75-billion-year-old universe appears to not be random at all, but rather precisely directed toward the creation of human life. Consider the entire natural world as we know it and how the elements and phenomena in it interact. The constants and values attached to them are not a coincidence. If the values of the gravitational force, electromagnetic field, nuclear strong force, or nuclear weak force were even slightly different, life as we know it would not exist.

Our planet has been precisely designed and fine-tuned to sustain life. It's not a void of nothingness or any kind of cosmic soup that brought us into existence in this way. This is the work of a creative mind that is beyond our concept of genius. I believe God, who was the beginning of all things, created a miraculous universe for us, and it is a powerful testament to and proof of His glory. Our amazing universe bears His signature. And He holds it all together and will be with us the whole way through. In Revelation 22:13, God says, "I am the Alpha and the Omega, the First and the Last, the Beginning and the End." He Himself is the most extraordinary constant of the universe.

When it comes to understanding our universe and the natural order of things, remember that science and faith do not always have to be at odds with one another. At the same time, I've heard it said that while philosophers and theologians study *what* God did and *why* He did it, scientists seek to figure out *how* He did it. In scientists' efforts to explain and understand the beginnings of the universe, their theories about creation sometimes change. But theologians trust and are unchanging in their belief that God created the universe. God tells us in Malachi 3:6, "I the Lord do not change." Hebrews 13:8 says, "Jesus Christ is the same yesterday and today and forever." Who God is has always been constant and will continue to be for all of eternity. I'm grateful we can depend on Him and know that He is God over all.

God's Moon

Never changing,
always there.
You make me feel
I want to stare.
A gift of beauty
That knows no cares.
Your paleness glistens against the dark.
Tonight you're mine; you've made your mark.
How many ages have had these thoughts?
How many times have you been sought?
My years are short and yours are many.
Then, one day there are not any.
To know what all you have seen,
such wisdom mankind could glean.
But, we are simple and seem not to learn.
With all we have, should we still yearn?
Content we are in our pathetic ways.
We live not realizing our few numbered days.
In the end we all must pray
our God of mercy, we can persuade.

—*Rhonda Dawes Milner*

CHAPTER 3

God's Intelligence and Genius

He determines the number of the stars and calls
them each by name. Great is our Lord and mighty
in power; his understanding has no limit.

PSALM 147:4–5

YOU MAY HAVE HEARD OF GOD DESCRIBED AS OMNISCIENT, meaning He knows everything and possesses all understanding of the universe—past, present, and future. He can see things in their totality, and His knowledge is limitless. As the One who made the world and everything in it, He also created knowledge itself. I believe signs of His intelligence and genius have been deeply ingrained in all created things, not only in nature but also in us.

Whether through the complicated design of the systems of the human body, the intricate sequencing of elements in nature, or the deliberate provision of natural resources necessary for human survival, God demonstrates a superior intelligence that's far beyond what any person could produce. I think it's incredible to observe how God's creation has His signature all over it and reveals the mastermind who made it.

In 1907, a doctor named Duncan MacDougall weighed tuberculosis patients before and after death. He found a 21-gram difference, something that to me is consistent with the idea that energy cannot be created or destroyed, only transformed.

On my first day in gross anatomy as a first-year medical student, it was confirmed for me that there's an invisible essence or energy of a person that gives the person life and leaves their body at death. The cadaver my team was assigned was an older woman who had smoked and passed away from lung cancer. Our professor instructed us to command ourselves in a respectful, honoring manner, remembering that the cadavers before us had been living human beings who had given their bodies to science to help us learn. It was sobering, and I felt sad and at the same time privileged that this woman was placed in my care. One moment there is life, the next moment death. One moment our lungs are filling with air and our hearts are beating spontaneously; then, they stop. The experience made me even more keenly aware of how death hovers over us. Does it suck our lives away or does it free our souls? When death comes, it leaves the empty, tangible shell of our body; but what a wonder the human body is when it is full of its life force. As we studied the many systems of this woman's body, I was in awe of the miraculous design behind them. I praised God for His work of glory. Surely, we are fearfully and wonderfully made!

The Human Body

The complexity and sophistication of the human body is amazing. All the parts of our body, its systems, and its functions work together simultaneously and miraculously, as if they've been designed to work that way. We have features and abilities that demonstrate genius beyond what our minds could ever conceive of or create.

The Bible says in Psalm 139:13–14, "For you created my inmost being; you knit me together in my mother's womb. I praise you because I am fearfully and wonderfully made; your works are wonderful, I know that full well." When we consider the elaborateness of the parts and systems of our bodies, I believe it's nearly impossible to ignore the intelligent design that went into it.

Our Cells

Even at the most cellular level is evidence of an intentional arrangement, with every feature playing an integral part. The cell itself has a permeable membrane around it, allowing it to absorb the nutrients it needs in order to survive. It was designed to have mitochondria inside, for producing energy. The nucleus of the cell, with deoxyribonucleic acid (DNA), serves as the brain of the cell, and within this is our genetic coding. The spiral-double helix of DNA in the cell contains all of our genetic information. And messenger ribonucleic acid (RNA) and transfer RNA also work within the cell. Francis Collins, a physician-geneticist recognized for his important discoveries of disease genes and his leadership of the Human Genome Project, observes in his book *The Language of God* that evidence for God is found in the intricacy and genius of this protein structure, the spiral-double helix of DNA.[1]

The glycoproteins, called laminins, are found in cells. They are part of the cellular basement membrane and are also the natural adhesives of cells. Laminins cause cells to be "sticky" so that adjacent cells can hold together with each other to form tissue. These tiny laminins are what literally hold us together and keep us from falling apart. Under an electron microscope, the laminin structure is shaped like a cross. How amazing God is to have the tiniest of cross-shaped cellular structures be fundamental in holding us together. This is another example of something in the natural world that points to God as the artist and Creator. Just as laminins do for the human body, is it not the Cross of Christ that holds a person together and keeps us from falling apart? God has signed His name on His creation, even on the tiny cells in our body.

Our Body's Systems

God has also miraculously designed our bodies to function with everything in sync and in complete coordination. The biological systems of our bodies, which sustain us and keep us alive, do innumerable things simultaneously and almost always without conscious effort on our part. A master plan built right into us speaks to the genius of a Creator.

The circulatory system, for example, is an extensive network of organs and vessels in charge of the flow of blood, nutrients, gases, and hormones to and from our cells. It carries what we need for life to every part of our bodies. Without this system, we wouldn't be able to fight off disease or regulate our bodies internally. As part of this system, our heart is the strongest muscle in the body, never fatiguing. How is it that God made it to never stop beating all our lives?

Our hematopoietic (blood) system itself is ingenious. Hemoglobin, inside our trillions of red blood cells, is a complex masterpiece that takes oxygen from our lungs to all the tissues in our body. Without it, we wouldn't be able to breathe. We're also able to keep from hemorrhaging because our blood was designed to clot. This is something that would be easy to take for granted but is truly a complex process. It's called the coagulation cascade and requires twelve steps, each of which needs to happen in perfect sequence. When we first receive an injury, our blood vessels contract, then platelets clump together to make a plug, and then a fibrin clot occurs through this intricate and precise coagulation cascade. The entire process is called hemostasis and, miraculously, stops us from bleeding to death. And though you wouldn't know it, the small range of our blood pH that is needed to sustain our life is a narrow, finely tuned, and balanced window that remains constant. Just as God designed the universe and keeps it in balance, He designed the blood system, only one of many systems in our body, to be intricate, precise, and perfect in function so that we could live.

Our skeletal system was designed with bones that enable us to move, stand, run, and eat. Without them to stabilize our body, we would be like jellyfish—without structure. But besides that, God created the inside of our bones with marrow so that the marrow could be used to create blood products. Bone marrow, part of our hematopoietic system, manufactures our blood cells, showing that God, in His grand design, does not waste any part of our bodies. The different functions of our body, even across different systems, work together as a whole.

Our respiratory system supplies oxygen for our body to keep us living. We can breathe with effort or automatically, voluntary or involuntary, respectively. At night, when we are sound asleep, our body keeps on breathing effortlessly. When you fully consider it all, it's amazing that the beautiful and intentional design of our bodies keeps us living.

I'm not even scratching the surface of the amazing biology of our bodies in this book, but consider a few of these other examples of God's genius—things that only He, as an omniscient God, would have the foreknowledge and wisdom to build into our bodies:

- Our immune system, with its macrophages, T cells, B cells, cytokines, and immunoglobulins, combines countless elements together in order to destroy foreign antigens, including the bacteria and viruses that constantly enter our body. Amazingly, it rids our bodies of cancer cells every day.

- Our intricate and complex reproductive system is not only about the creation of another human being but also the fascinating process of gene transmission. God designed somewhere around forty thousand genes in the human genome.

- Our well-planned digestive system, among other things, uses enzymes, bile, glycolysis, glycogenesis, and the Krebs cycle to convert our food intake to energy and body maintenance. It processes the food we consume and extracts all the nutrients we need, demonstrating our body's remarkable ability to take materials and find a way to use them so that we can function.

- Our skin, part of the integumentary system, covers and protects our body. It's able to regenerate itself as it gets damaged from the elements that it is exposed to. When you truly consider this fact, it's amazing that God made it so we are able, without any conscious effort on our part, to regenerate a damaged part of our own body.

- Another fascinating self-regulatory system is sleep, something we cannot live without and which is absolutely necessary in order for our bodies to function. The human body needs to sleep about a third of each day. Sleep is needed to restore and rejuvenate health, work with our immune system to heal us and remove toxins, download and process information in our brain, synthesize hormones, repair and grow tissue, and do so many other functions. Even much of our creativity and ingenuity comes in our sleep through our subconscious.

I could provide countless more examples of the wondrous nature of our bodies' systems. For me, the details, precision, and functions built into our biological systems are undeniably amazing. They work in tandem with one another in a way that would be difficult to perceive of as accidental, and I believe they are planned by a loving and all-knowing God.

Our Senses

Our bodies' senses are also a display of God's genius. As humans, we experience life through our senses, and they allow us to discover and interact with our surroundings in rich, complex ways. They enable us to survive, and each one works together with the other senses to allow our brains to take in information and know what is going on around us. We recognize when we see something beautiful or appreciate when we taste something delicious, but how often do we pause and truly marvel at the wonder of our senses?

Take our sense of sight, for example. Think about the eye and the way it works. One of the most complex parts of our body, it consists of more than two million working parts and is the fastest moving muscle we have. It's an intricately designed system that coordinates with our brain to process images, and, amazingly, is made mostly of water.

Our sense of hearing depends on tiny hairs inside our ears. Hearing is an intricate process coordinated with the brain that allows us to distinguish sounds and understand words. Our ears help us to balance, and they're always working, even when we're asleep. Because of the way our brains process sound, we can hear music and recognize the beauty in it. Some composers even write music after hearing completed compositions in their minds.

Our sense of smell, or olfactory system, allows us to take in fragrances and odors. The sensory cells in our nose are connected directly to our brain. In fact, our sense of smell is closely linked with our memory. We have about six million odor-detecting cells, and our scent cells renew every month. When the sensory cells in our noses are stimulated by a smell in the environment around us, they send a message to the brain. It's extraordinary to think of the way our nose and brain work together to process a smell and trigger a response or reaction to it.

Much of our sense of taste also happens through our nose. And as with sensory cells in our nose, the sensory cells on our tongue transport information to our brain. A flavor is not only processed by our brain but also evokes an emotional response. We need our senses of smell and taste to ensure that we feed ourselves in order to live. But we're also able to better understand and interact with our surroundings based on the emotional responses triggered by our brain.

Our skin, part of our sense of touch, was specifically made to contain nerve endings and pain receptors. We have more receptors for pain than for any other sensation. Although one might think that a loving God would not subject His loved ones to pain, in His brilliance and foresight, He knew we would need to be able to sense pain as a protective device for our bodies. When we detect pain, we remove ourselves from its source, which could otherwise damage our body in some way. Even the idea of nerve endings in our skin was designed by God to protect our survival.

All of our senses interact with our brain, the most complex and miraculous organ of the human body. The neurological system, composed of all our nerves, spinal cord, and brain, is an intricate and complex computer system. Considering only a few of the brain's abilities—the thought process, the imagination process, the ability to learn, or the neuroplasticity required for us to adapt and change—the brain becomes astounding and difficult to comprehend. The brain is what controls our ability to move, eat, sleep, and talk. It sends billions of signals throughout our body to make our systems function and allow for every action. It also enables us to think, create, learn, and feel. Our brain produces enough electricity to power a light bulb, and it processes faster than any computer. And perhaps most importantly, it helps us to make decisions and know how we should go about living life. Another thing God did for us is to make prayer and meditation one of the best activities we can do for our brains; these not only produce feelings of well-being but also can increase our health and longevity.

God gifted us with our senses and an amazing brain; built intentionally into our biology, they allow us to know Him. They are essential for our survival, and they enable us to function more effectively in life. In their purpose and composition, they are evidence once again of a grand design.

Everything in the human body is pure genius. I believe in the old adage: If we see a watch, there must be a watchmaker. Scientists and doctors note a design present in our human bodies. It seems impossible to ignore the intricacy of our making. At the same time, we're made of more than just skin, bones, and cells; we're not just biology or anatomical function. We've been given souls that make us human and remind us that we're beloved.

Mathematical Sequencing in Nature

God's genius is evident in more than just the human body. Scientists and mathematicians have found a fascinating mathematical sequencing built right into nature. It's repeated everywhere and is something you've probably even observed without knowing it.

The Fibonacci sequence begins like this: 0, 1, 1, 2, 3, 5, 8, 13, 21, 34, 55, etc. In this sequence, each number is the sum of the two numbers that precede it. It has a special relationship with what's known as the golden ratio (also referred to by its Greek letter "phi"), which is a specific ratio or distribution in geometry. This ratio is used in art, architecture, and design, and some say that it makes the most aesthetically appealing shape. Fibonacci numbers appear in nature often enough that they point to the work of a grand Designer. They can be found in fruits, vegetables, plants, flowers, sunflower seeds, spider webs, bees, chameleon tails, snail shells, seashells, the ocean, whirlpools, hurricanes, and even the human body. I believe that these are operating universal laws that God has designed to create order and meaning. These natural phenomena· point to a Creator, a divine master-organizer of the universe.

Within the plant world, these sequences and ratios are seen in the branching of stems and limbs as well as in the patterns of florets seen in flowers. They are present in the arrangement of a pinecone, the scales of a pineapple, the flowering of an artichoke, and the uncurling of a fern.

Besides being visible in the arrangement of the branching of stems, the golden ratio can be seen in the skeletal pattern of bones, the branching of nerves and veins, the geometry of crystals, in deoxyribonucleic acid (DNA), and in chemical compounds. It is applicable to the growth of every living thing.

The symmetry and proportions that the sequencing and ratios produce appear to our eye as beauty, and they represent all the beauty in nature, with its pinnacle realized in the human form. They are part of a numbering system, observable by anyone, that appears everywhere and offers empirical evidence of a master Creator. This numbering system demonstrates great planning and foresight in design, and when we examine the beauty, symmetry, and sequencing closely, it would seem difficult to ignore that there's something greater at play. The order and sequencing God built into nature and the natural world is pure genius. God's signature appears mathematically and organically, and He uses these attributes to benefit us as people but also to show us He's there.

Order for Our Existence

God planned it all. With the kind of genius and creativity that only He is capable of, He also designed the natural world to support and further our existence. He provides what we need for our survival, wasting nothing. Consider a few of these examples of the intricacy and brilliance of His plan:

- Animals and plants provide us with food.

- Not only did God provide plants as a food source, but also the oxygen by-product of photosynthesis supplements our own oxygen supply. Plants help supply the very air we breathe.

- God gives us the water we need through rain, lakes, rivers, streams, and springs. The water cycle He created sustains all living things.

- Trees, rocks, and other natural resources provide shelter for us.

- Flint rocks, created by God to possess the qualities they have, offer a way for people to create fire, something that changed life for the earliest humans. Fire not only offered people a way to keep warm and cook food but also, through its innumerable effects, changed the course of history.

- God made the mold and fungi used to produce penicillin, which has saved countless lives.

- God created all the elements that make up our world, including carbon, hydrogen, and oxygen, elements fundamental to all organic life.

- Amino acids, the fundamental building blocks of our bodies, are God's idea.

He also creates ways for plants and trees to survive, continue, and flourish. I believe nature reveals God's genius in the concept of a small seed or an acorn. These are perfect little packages designed to produce a variety of plant life and the greatest of trees. How did God design something so small to contain all the information necessary to produce living, growing plants and trees that are so large compared to their origin? It is amazing to think that all the beauty of a flower is contained in the smallest of seeds. God also designed the seeds to be resilient and to survive harsh conditions until they have been planted and have proper conditions to germinate. This is particularly clever when one considers the importance our food source has to our survival as a species.

The likelihood of any of these intricate systems coming into existence on their own as a random or chance occurrence is difficult to imagine, especially when we observe a universe that tends to disorder. In fact, all of the systems God created—whether in our human bodies, in mathematical sequencing and symmetry in nature, or as resources used for our survival—demonstrate a well-orchestrated plan and level of intelligence far superior to any intellect. There is an orderly arrangement and a design present, a signature made by an all-knowing, omniscient being.

Why did He do all this for us? I would imagine for myriad reasons but maybe to guarantee our well-being and existence. Maybe so that we would know Him through His creation and understand that He loves us.

The Bible states in 1 John 3:19–20, "This is how we know that we belong to the truth and how we set our hearts at rest in His presence. If our hearts condemn us, we know that God is greater than our hearts and he knows everything." God knows why He made the world for us in precisely the way He did. I'm thankful for a loving Creator who knows us through and through, knows what we need, and has not only the genius and foresight to make it but also the willingness to do so.

God's Design

God created a perfect, sublime design
Born into the dimensions of space and time

Cells with secret helix keys to life
All contained within, enough to suffice

Inhale, exhale motions always there
God has done all this with His loving care

Hearts with unceasing perpetual beats
Never a moment's rest, respite, or defeat

Imagination, thoughts, music roam in the mind
Curiosity, intelligence, wondering answers to find

Dreaming cloudy visions, slumbering quiet sleep
Brings healing to the body and soul for us to keep

Prayers and faith play their infinite part
Keeping us healthy, well, close to God's heart

Programmed to physically one day die
He holds all these answers, the reasons why

God wired us like Him for loving others
He created us to be all sisters and brothers

So in His creation, design, and plan
He made us into miracles by His hands

—*Rhonda Dawes Milner*

CHAPTER 4

God's Power and Strength

All power is given unto me in heaven and in earth.

MATTHEW 28:18 (KJV)

GOD CREATED THE UNIVERSE, SO IT TELLS OF HIS SOVER-
eignty, power, and character. And He signed His name in the natural
world in such a way that it offers, among His other incredible attributes,
His strength. We can see the sun and the moon, the stars and the sky, but
who had the power to put these in place? Who has the strength to hold
the world together? I believe not only that God's creation displays His
power and strength but also that His power and strength in creation help
us better understand and know Him.

The amount of power we can witness in His creation is overwhelm-
ing. I can't even begin to grasp the kind of power God must have had
to create the universe and to sustain it now. The Bible tells us in Job
26:7–14 (NLT):

> God stretches the northern sky over empty space and
> hangs the earth on nothing. He wraps the rain in his

thick clouds, and the clouds don't burst with the weight. He covers the face of the moon, shrouding it with his clouds. He created the horizon when he separated the waters: he set the boundary between day and night. The foundations of heaven tremble; they shudder at his rebuke. By his power the sea grew calm. By his skill he crushed the great sea monster. His Spirit made the heavens beautiful, and his power pierced the gliding serpent. These are just the beginning of all that he does, merely a whisper of his power. Who, then, can comprehend the thunder of his power?

As this verse and Matthew 28:18, the verse at the beginning of the chapter, reveal, God is unlimited in His capabilities and has complete power and authority over everything in Heaven and the natural world. He is omnipotent, an almighty, all-powerful God. I'll show you a few ways in which His power is displayed in nature and the animal kingdom and also talk about what His strength means for us personally.

God's Power and Strength in Nature

Nature is full of examples of God's power—the intimidating presence of a mighty mountain, the brilliant and terrifying flash of lightning, the violent shaking of ground during an earthquake. God communicates things about Himself through nature that we wouldn't otherwise be able to understand. Even the enormity of a tidal wave says something about who He is.

The ocean, a force in its own, is so colossal, vast, and powerful that its mere existence points to a colossal, vast, and powerful Creator. Covering over 70 percent of our planet and exceeding the surface area of all combined landmasses, it stretches beyond the horizon and delves into the deepest depths. It can be peaceful and calm in one moment but then destructive enough to swallow entire ships or bring destruction to cities in another. The ocean contains an almost limitless amount of energy in its waves. It also houses an enormous world beneath its surface, with its own creatures, organisms, plant life, geography, resources, mysteries, and phenomena. Did you know that the earth's longest mountain range is in the ocean? That more than 90 percent of all volcanic activity happens underwater? That the coral found in the ocean is so similar to human bone that it's sometimes used for bone repair?

The ocean is fed by streams and rivers, which flow down from mountain springs. In the allegorical novel *Hinds' Feet on High Places*, author Hannah Hurnard speaks of water from mountains flowing down from high places to low places, highlighting that water flows from many streams and rivers to the ocean to form one body.[1] This body represents the body of Christ, coming from many to form one. I love that the ocean points to God and His attributes, even from metaphorical and topographical standpoints.

As well, earth, in the beginning, was completely covered by water. The Bible says in Genesis 1:1–2, the first two verses of the Bible, that when God created the heavens and the earth and the earth was still formless and empty, "The Spirit of God was hovering over the waters." And Revelation 22:13 says, "I am the Alpha and Omega, the First and the Last, the Beginning and the End." God was here in the very beginning and will be here to the end. The world started with and ends with Him. He is the source, just as springs are the source of rivers that end in the ocean.

Even other water on our planet serves to tell of who God is. His power, strength, beauty, and glory can be seen in magnificent waterfalls, like Victoria Falls and Niagara Falls. Water is so powerful it can be used to run hydroelectric plants and provide energy to cities. We use water every day, and for me, it's incredible to realize that the power of water can reveal the power of God.

In nature, storms and natural disasters also speak of His might. Hurricanes, tsunamis, tornadoes, earthquakes, volcanic explosions, landslides, avalanches, and blizzards can be horrific events; and even as we experience tremendous loss from these natural phenomena, we also glimpse something of God's power in them. Storms and natural disasters, most of which are weather related, can be incredibly scary and violent. Their capacity for mass destruction is not to be trifled with. The Old Testament speaks of the wrath of God, and though we should remember that He is good and everything He does in the world is consistent with His goodness, these calamities in nature still demonstrate a terrifying kind of power and strength.

God reveals His character through nature—good *and* bad. Storms and natural disasters show us a side of God that has to do with judgment, too. Does He love us? Absolutely. Will He help us in the face of disaster? No question. But Christians believe we also live in a world that has the effects of original sin. Natural disasters are, in a sense, a ripple effect of that, and life on this side of Heaven is not without calamities like this happening.

I believe God can use nature to help and teach us. It can bless us and also challenge us. He still extends a gracious power to us through nature, and in the same way He is in control of nature, He is also in control of taking care of us. Nature reveals God's power, and it's up to us to trust His power and strength and also His goodness and love in it.

God's Power and Strength in the Animal Kingdom

God created animals to inhabit the earth with us. I believe that in their design they point the way to His power. Only God would have the authority and ability to make so many creatures and organisms with as much creativity, artistry, and knowledge as He did.

I also believe that animals matter because they matter to God. The Bible tells us in the book of Genesis that God designated a specific day of creation for making animals, and when He later viewed everything He had made, He declared it all to be "very good." In the time of the Flood, also described in Genesis, God specifically saved the animals from drowning. This shows that God is engaged with *all* of His creation—in this case, animals—not only people. To me, even in their very existence, animals are a display of the life, beauty, and power that God intentionally brought into our world.

Symbolically, in the animal kingdom the lion is often referred to as the "king of beasts." He has power over all other animals because of His strength, and His mighty roar represents power and control over the entire animal kingdom. This role has been played out in literature and lore for centuries, including in C. S. Lewis's famous series *The Chronicles of Narnia,* in which he writes of Aslan, the lion. In the books, Aslan, the mighty, wise, and kind lion, is used to symbolize Christ. Lewis, himself a theologian, made a connection between the symbol of the lion in common thought and Christ, highlighting God's power, fortitude, and strength through Aslan.

God created the lion to have certain physical traits and an unmistakable presence. Though all animals have their origin in Him, the lion in particular is often linked to the idea of a leader or king. It is a picture of power.

The book of Revelation refers to God as the "Lion of Judah." This name speaks to a connection between the lion and Christ, once again showing that the power of one can be attributed to the other. Though the lion is the created thing, it points to its Creator.

The eagle is another analogy often used in illustrations about God because of its unique characteristics. It was created as a strong, bold-looking, high-flying bird with powerful vision. Large in size and known for its power, the eagle is at the top of its food chain. It is fearless and said not to ever surrender to its prey. People associate the eagle with leadership, power, mental strength, and clarity of vision, and for this reason it has been used symbolically by rulers for thousands of years.

In the Bible, the eagle serves as a symbol of the strength of God, sometimes even symbolizing Christ Himself. Psalm 91:4 says, "He will cover you with his feathers, and under his wings you will find refuge; his faithfulness will be your shield and rampart." Exodus 19:4 reads, "You yourselves have seen what I did to Egypt, and how I carried you on eagles' wings and brought you to myself." The eagle flies high above the other birds soaring in the sky; with its eagle eye, it can see all—the big picture from afar, as God sees the big picture. We are called to trust Him because He sees the big picture, and at all times—even when we are going through pain and suffering in life or need to make big decisions—He acts on our behalf, only doing what is best for us and helping us become the person He always created us to be.

As we've observed, the eagle is also powerful, a picture of strength. When we associate this power and strength with God, we come to understand Him as mighty and able to help us in any situation in life. God possesses these qualities, claims these attributes, and has placed them in the eagle so we could know these things about Him. In this, we can trust Him and put our faith in His power, ability, and genuine care for us.

The Bible says in Isaiah 40:31, "But those who hope in the Lord will renew their strength. They will soar on wings like eagles; they will run and not grow weary, they will walk and not be faint." God also uses the eagle to help us understand faith. In this verse, we are the eagle, and its wings represent our faith in God. The verse tells us that God, in His power, can replenish us and can give us strength. He is able to renew and restore us, giving us all we need to not only persevere but also soar. God uses the symbol of the eagle to help and encourage us. When we see or think about the eagle, we can see or think about Him and recognize it as His signature placed in the world for us.

God's Power and Strength in Us

Symbolic associations between God, nature, and animals can be uplifting and inspirational. These connections are intentional and a sign of His love for us and His power in the world. But these associations are only associations unless they truly inform or transform the way we live our lives. When we observe the evidence He's placed around us in nature or think about the way He's signed His name in the universe, we see things about our existence that we can't unsee. These things empower us, through His Holy Spirit, to believe in a Creator and live our lives differently.

Zechariah 4:6 says, "'Not by might, nor by power, but by My Spirit,' says the Lord." He is an omnipotent, all-powerful God, and we can trust in Him. But we won't be able to do this with our own strength, might, or power. This verse tells us that God will help us and realize all things in our lives through the power of His Holy Spirit. Isaiah 41:10 says, "So do not fear, for I am with you; do not be dismayed, for I am your God. I will strengthen you and help you; I will uphold you with my righteous hand." And in Philippians 4:13, the writer encourages us to rely on the strength of God, saying, "I can do all this through him who gives me strength."

God is the epitome of power and strength, and this has huge implications for our lives. When we trust in a powerful, capable God, our worries are gone, and we feel safe and protected. It's impossible to trust God at the same time that we worry, because if we worry, we are not trusting God. Ultimately, when we worry and have fears of situations or the future, we need to choose to remember who He is and all that He promises us; through the help of the Holy Spirit, we can turn those thoughts into trust and belief in our Father. No worry, problem, or fear is too big for God to handle. As an omnipotent God, He has the power to handle them all. And when we believe in Him, He gives us any amount of strength and power we need. In fact, supernaturally, the power of His Holy Spirit comes to rest in us. It's absolutely incredible to think that when we trust in Him, His power can be in us. Then, as it says in Philippians 4:7, "The peace of God, which transcends all understanding, will guard your hearts and your minds in Christ Jesus."

Only God in His power and strength can provide for us and take away every care and worry. Only in God's power and strength can we find our power and strength. Psalm 62:1–2 says, "Truly my soul finds rest in God; my salvation comes from him. Truly he is my rock and my salvation; he is my fortress, I will never be shaken." Think of these images of God's power: He is described as a "rock" and "fortress." Biblically, rocks are associated with strength. They're solid, unchanging, and used to build shelters, fortresses, and foundations. Fortresses protect us from danger and offer us safety from attack.

God is our refuge. When we believe this about Him, we find freedom in Him and experience spiritual and emotional rest in our souls. St. Augustine, an early Christian theologian and philosopher, says in his confessions that God made us for Himself, and our hearts will be restless until they find rest in Him.[2] Only God provides the rest our soul desires, and we can only find our strength through God's strength. When we turn our lives over to God, trusting in His loving care, a burden is lifted from us.

It's amazing that the God who was powerful enough to create the universe and everything in it—the mighty, omnipotent God—chooses to make Himself known to us in order to love us. As you continue to think about who He is and what this means for your life, take heart in the encouragement of Ephesians 6:10, "Be strong in the Lord and in his mighty power."

The Privilege

The cool water presses to my body like a wet wick.
Each breath is short and very quick
until it slows to the rhythm of my inborn beat.
It is deep down here that I, myself, first meet.
As I descend below the light
I see such creatures of delight.
The colors and the shapes that surround
bring awe and wonder without a sound.
I am here the stranger and am their guest.
There is nothing here I want to miss.
Deep down below brings true bliss.

This is a window to another world.
All God's power can unfurl.
His strength and might rest quietly in
such destruction disguised from within.
Floating slowly the time has passed.
This privilege is gone; it was too fast.
The magic vision disappears as I ascend.
I pray dear Lord to come again.

—*Rhonda Dawes Milner*

CHAPTER 5

God's Comfort and Presence

*As I was with Moses, so I will be with you; I
will never leave you nor forsake you.*

JOSHUA 1:5

IN THE BIBLE WHEN CHRIST ASCENDED INTO HEAVEN,
God sent His Holy Spirit to be with us. The Holy Spirit is to be our com-
forter and to reside with us. His presence helps us through fear, worry,
and distress. His presence is with us in moments of joy, contentment, and
calm. His presence offers us peace, meaning, and purpose. I believe that
God has made Himself manifest in His natural world in order to give us
hope and comfort in our lives. Whether through our experiences with
animals or nature, His presence assures us that we are not alone, that
He is with us in each moment, and that He is actively engaged in the
circumstances of our lives.

Psalm 118:27 says, "The Lord is God, and he has made his light shine
upon us." John 16:33 tells us, "I have told you these things, so that in
me you may have peace. In this world you will have trouble. But take

heart! I have overcome the world." In the coming pages, I'll share some of my own personal experiences and observations about God's comfort and presence in the natural world and talk about what this might mean for you. Whether we realize it or not, God shows His favor to us through His creation. His signature in the natural world says a lot about who He is and how He feels about us.

God's Comfort and Presence in Animals

God works in our lives through animals. Whether through the dove sent out by Noah from the ark (Genesis 8); the grasshoppers, flies, and frogs used in the plagues (Exodus 8 and 10); the whale that enveloped Jonah (Jonah 1–2); or the lions forbidden from attacking Daniel (Daniel 6), God used these and other animals to carry out His purposes. In accounts from the Bible as well as in our own personal lives, animals remind us that God is there. I've found that He often uses animals to comfort and help us; and through them, we experience a little more of who He is.

For example, in my life and in so many people's lives, dogs are our comforters. They show us an unconditional love we don't always deserve, something that points to what God does for us on a much larger scale. They accept us the way we are, as God accepts us. And they are always by our side, just as God is always with us, never forsaking us. Dogs give us love and are faithful in their devotion to us. For people who may be alone in life, never having experienced genuine love from someone else, their dog may be the only picture of unconditional love they will ever see, and it may be their only opportunity to understand how God loves people. I believe God gave us companion animals to demonstrate something of His comfort and love, so we may know more about Him.

Besides companionship, dogs also act on our behalf to help and comfort us. At one time or another you may have encountered news stories or met people who have these kinds of experiences with their dogs:

- Dogs barking and awakening their families in the middle of the night in order to alert them about house fires or burglaries

- Dogs being trained to save their owners from deadly food allergies

- Seizure-assistance dogs, able to detect oncoming seizures, saving the lives of their owners by providing advance notice

- Guide dogs and hearing dogs, helping owners with specific impairments

- Mobility-assistance dogs that help enable their wheel-chair-bound owners to perform more tasks and be more independent

- Autism-assistance dogs, providing safety, emotional support, and companionship to their owners

- Dogs that are trained to sniff out bombs to save lives

Dogs are wonderful animals for many reasons, including helping to promote their owners' health and well-being. God uses them to bless us, and as an extension of His care, they show us care. In doing so, we are shown comfort in difficulty and offered something of His presence through His creation.

My oldest son, now deceased, would tell the story of when, during his early college years, he recognized that his drinking and partying were getting out of hand. He happened to think one day of how much he loved and admired his grandfather and recalled that he prayed to God to make him into the kind of man his grandfather would be proud of. The following week, when he was consuming wine one night and letting his dog out, the dog ran off. Strangely, though his dog had been with him for many years, it had never before attempted to run away. Caught off guard, my son immediately ran outside with the glass of wine in his hand, calling for his dog. This was when a policeman who had been patrolling the neighborhood saw my underage son. My son was charged with underage drinking, an incident that put the brakes on his behavior, taught him to control himself, and ultimately helped him to get his life back on track. He believed God intervened through his dog to help him out of a bad life situation at a time when he could not help himself out of it. He clearly saw God's help and presence in the incident and connected his dog's actions with God's will. The day he shared his experience, he said something I had never thought of: that "dog" spelled backward is "God." This is a special story that I cherish about my son; I'm touched and moved by the gratitude he had for God's intervention in his life.

Another of God's creatures that comes to mind is the dove. Biblically and symbolically, the white dove has great significance. In John 1:32–34,

John says, "I saw the Spirit come down from heaven as a dove and remain on him. And I myself did not know him, but the One who sent me to baptize with water told me, 'The man on whom you see the Spirit come down and remain is the one who will baptize with the Holy Spirit.' I have seen and I testify that this is God's Chosen One." Matthew 3:16–17 reads, "As soon as Jesus was baptized, he went up out of the water. At that moment heaven was opened, and he saw the Spirit of God descending like a dove and alighting on Him. And a voice from heaven said, 'This is my Son, whom I love; with Him I am well pleased.'" These passages show that God chose the white dove to portray and embody the Holy Spirit.

The dove has come over time to be recognized around the world as a symbol of peace. It's often portrayed with an olive branch in its beak, which is a direct connection to the historical account of Noah found in Genesis 8. We associate the dove with serenity, harmony, tranquility, and calm. It's a messenger of peace and order, and a white dove in particular is connected to the idea of purity. This creature communicates the peace, comfort, and presence of God; and through it, we are inspired and reminded more of what He is about.

We also know from the Bible that after Christ ascended into Heaven, God sent the Holy Spirit on the day of Pentecost to comfort us and help us know Him. In Acts 1:4–5, Jesus gave the command, "Do not leave Jerusalem, but wait for the gift my Father promised, which you have heard me speak about. For John baptized with water, but in a few days you will be baptized with the Holy Spirit." God wants us to have His comfort and presence. He wants us to live our lives with the comfort and help He provides.

Whether physically, emotionally, or symbolically, animals can be used to bless us and carry out God's will. I encourage you to look for the Creator and His amazing attributes in them. See what you might be able to learn or discover about God in your life through them.

God's Comfort and Presence in Nature

God provides comfort, peace, and a sense of well-being through nature. He does this through the coolness of a breeze, the sound of the surf, the beauty of a mountain, the stillness of a cloud, or the smell of a grassy field. I can't help but experience a sense of gratefulness during these times. They're like gifts from God to pull me back from heavier, harder things in life and to remind me He's there.

For me, the sun has a special way of making me feel God's comfort and constant presence. I know God is always with me, and yet to see the sunrise in the morning is an intimate and joyful experience, like God saying, "Good morning. Here I am," to me. It's as if He's welcoming me into the day and inviting me to be with Him because He wants to be with me.

In the daytime, I believe He is there, represented in the sun, shining in amazing beauty, brightly and brilliantly waiting for us to notice and enjoy His presence. I feel the warmth of His touch. I witness the way He enables things to grow. I see things by His light.

And in the evenings, if I'm able to catch a magnificent sunset, to witness the sun sinking into the horizon and then vanishing, I feel a sense of peace and well-being, a reminder of God's constant love. We don't see the sun as it sinks below the horizon, but it is still shining there, ever present and unfailing. This is as God is during those times when we feel we can't see Him: He is there, constant, emanating light, glorious. The same is true when we don't see the sun on a rainy, foggy, or overcast day. We may be in a rainy, dark, or overcast time in our lives, but I'm grateful to know the Son exists nonetheless—and simply because we may not be able to see Him does not mean He's not working. I hate to miss a sunset or sunrise and the reminders and simple, quiet reassurances of His love and presence. They put things in perspective and direct my gaze to Him.

I heard a story once of a prisoner in a Nazi concentration camp who felt that the sun had a similar impact on him. The man knew that on the many dark days when he could not see the sun, it was still there. Though his time in the camp was full of unspeakable horror, he looked to the sun as a reminder that God had not forsaken him. He knew that God was still there, that God had not turned His back on him, that God still lived. For him, the sun offered hope, comfort, and a palpable reminder of God's presence. And I believe God used the sun to inspire that hope and help in the man.

How do we trust in God's comfort and presence as this man did? How do God's peace and presence within us help and inform the way we see our situations and live our lives? God has always revealed facets of who He is through His creation—He has lovingly, miraculously, intricately signed His name on the natural world—and if we're able to view these clues and symbols with different eyes, even in the most difficult of situations, we're better able to see Him.

God's Comfort and Presence in Us

Whether we have faith in God or not, His comfort and presence are what our souls truly long for. We may find significant comfort in other people, situations, or things, but the Bible tells us that only He can provide this kind of deep, lasting, unfailing satisfaction for our souls. Because of who He is and what we know and experience of His attributes, a relationship with Him is the only one that will never ultimately disappoint, the only one that will never fail. This does not discount the other people or circumstances in our lives; in fact, as we've discussed in this book, we can experience tremendous comfort in His creation because He made them to reflect His love. But as the unfailing, omniscient, omnipotent, omnipresent God of the universe, His is the only love, comfort, and help that is perfect. He has known about you since before He created the world, He made the world with you in mind, He shaped the circumstances and contexts of your life specifically and for a reason, and He promises His presence to you always. God tells us in Jeremiah 31:3, "I have loved you with an everlasting love; I have drawn you with unfailing kindness." In God, you will always have a comfort, hope, peace, and perspective that transcend any situations.

God's Comfort and Presence in Our Pain and Suffering

I once read about a woman who had experienced tremendous hurt and loss in her life. She believed difficult things sometimes take us so far down in life that the only way to see is up; and it's in these times that we see Him. Have you ever felt so deep in the bottom of a dark hole in your pain, suffering, or grief that you weren't sure where to look? The place to find light is up. Suffering gets our attention in a way that other situations might not. When we suffer and grieve, we're more receptive to and keenly aware of God's presence. When we're at the end of ourselves, we can find light in the face of Jesus. When we are at our weakest and most vulnerable is when we look for hope from a source greater than we are. God says in 2 Corinthians 12:9, "My grace is sufficient for you, for my power is made perfect in weakness." When we are in pain, God meets us in a personal, powerful, comforting way. He wants for us to realize that we need to rely on and find our help in Him, and when we trust Him in our pain, He offers us His amazing and supernatural comfort.

In my pain and suffering in losing my son in 2011, I felt God draw me close to Him under His wing. In our brokenness, God opens us up to Him to receive His love. He cries with us in our grief and loss. In those tender months following my son's death, I probably never felt closer to God in His loving arms. I experienced many supernatural experiences of God's love and presence, making me aware that our love and our loved ones live on. After my son died, I asked God for a sign that my son was with Him. He sent me a beautiful red cardinal, and I knew all was well.

In *The Pursuit of God*, pastor, author, and teacher A. W. Tozer says that when religion has the last word, all we really need is God Himself; and in Him, we will find what we have secretly been longing for all our lives.[1] We need God's presence, and as deeply in pain as we may feel we are at times, God's love can always be deeper still. Even when we're not aware that we long for Him, He seeks to fill our need.

In his book *The Problem of Pain*, author, scholar, and theologian C. S. Lewis says that God shouts to us in our pain to get our attention.[2] God may speak more softly to us in other life situations, but He recognizes that when we're in pain, we really need to hear Him and know He's there. He does not want us to miss it; He cares that much about our pain.

In the poem "Dark Night of the Soul," sixteenth-century mystic and poet John of the Cross writes to us about times in our lives when we feel that God has abandoned us. He says that in these times of spiritual desolation when we are almost inconsolable, God is making a space within us so we are able to come into union with Him so He can be closer to us than ever.[3] God never wastes an ounce of our suffering. He will use it to draw us near to Him. In those "dark nights of the soul" when life feels painful and hopeless, God is waiting with us and by us in the darkness. He does not leave us alone to suffer but is waiting for us to reach out into the darkness in faith to find His open hand; His hand is ready to receive ours and guide us out of the darkness into the safety of His light.

When we believe, God gives us an incredible comfort. As His creation, He is always working on our behalf. He's with us whether we know Him or not and whether we choose Him or not. But until we reach out in faith, we will not be able to know the fullness of His presence, the depth of His comfort, or the light and glory of Christ in our hearts. In 2 Corinthians 4:6 we read, "For God, who said, 'Let light shine out of darkness,' made his light shine in our hearts to give us the light of the knowledge of God's glory displayed in the face of Christ."

God has left clues everywhere in His natural creation and signed His name on it for us to see. He wants us to know there is no deeper satisfaction than knowing Him and being in His presence. Jeremiah 29:11–14 says, "'For I know the plans I have for you,' declares the Lord, 'plans to prosper you and not to harm you, plans to give you hope and a future. Then you will call on me and come and pray to me, and I will listen to you. You will seek me and find me when you seek me with all your heart. I will be found by you,' declares the Lord . . . 'and will bring you back to the place which I carried you into exile.'"

God will comfort you. In Him, you have help, hope, and a future. He extends this to you and makes His presence available to everyone. How comforting to know that He reaches out to provide peace and hope to a hurting world.

God Is There

God's presence is seen everywhere
The sun, our source, gives us life
The solid, unmovable earth exists for us to stand
The gentle breeze whispers God's name
The lightning bolt gives light into darkness
The gale force winds display His power and might
The details of each and every
snowflake show His creativity
The restorative rain replenishes
and brings new growth
The blue, yellow, and burnt-orange skies
reveal His artistry
The lush valleys, vast oceans, still waters, and mighty
mountains exhibit His grandeur
All God's metaphors give testimony to His plan

I turn to the right; I turn to the left
I look above; I look below
I look all around
God is there, everywhere, waiting to be found

—*Rhonda Dawes Milner*

CHAPTER 6

God's Glory and Majesty

*Hallelujah! For our Lord God Almighty reigns. Let
us rejoice and be glad and give Him glory!*

REVELATION 19:6–7

GOD'S GLORY AND MAJESTY ARE DIFFICULT TO DESCRIBE.
There are simply no words that could adequately explain these aspects of
God in all their fullness. Glory entails everything amazing about God's
character. Majesty speaks to His sovereignty, greatness, and authority.
But even our best thinking, studying, worship, or praise could not cap-
ture all of who He is.

We do, however, have an awareness of His glory and majesty because
of the way He manifests Himself in our lives. In the Old Testament, He
at times made His glory visible or observable, appearing as a cloud, fire,
or smoke. And we can still see physical signs of His glory today. In fact,
all of creation reveals His glory and majesty, a gracious thing He's done
that allows us to know Him and to understand we're loved. We see examples of who He is in creation, and even as we may be limited in our ability
to articulate the power and emotional resonance of these in our lives, we
witness and are blessed by them nonetheless.

In the coming pages, I'll share some observations and inspirations about God's glory and majesty in creation. Because these so often exist as God's signature around us, I suspect that you have seen or experienced similar types of revelations in your own life. I love knowing that He uses them to draw us close to Him.

Nature and Our Sensibilities

In the Bible, Psalm 19:1 tells us, "The heavens declare the glory of God; the skies proclaim the work of his hands." Psalm 29:3 says, "The voice of the Lord is over the waters; the God of glory thunders, the Lord thunders over the mighty waters." God has chosen to display His glory and majesty to us through His creation. I believe He does this in beautiful, magnificent ways all the time, offering us a chance to engage with Him.

Have you ever stood somewhere high, somewhere with a breathtaking view of nature that makes you pause as you take in the scene around you? Maybe you're on a mountaintop or hill, looking out over miles of trees in a valley or the expanse of clouds in the sky. Maybe the colors in the sky at dawn or dusk cause you to catch your breath or make you feel humble. Maybe you're in the middle of a boat, realizing how vast and blue and limitless the water is and how small you are. At such times you are seeing nature bear witness to God's glory or recognizing how seemingly insignificant you are in comparison to the greatness of beauty and enormity of creation He's placed before you. Without knowing it, you might be feeling the awe of God's majesty or observing something that moves you and points you to God's glory.

You can experience Him in a rolling green pasture, a field of wildflowers, the petals in a rose, the flowing leaves of a weeping willow. You can find His grandeur and magnificence in the light sparkling on a mountain brook, the song of a nightingale, a herd of wild horses running free, the glistening exquisiteness of falling snow, a soft summer rain. You can discover His radiance in the early morning chatter of birds, the hatching of an egg, a harvest moon, a star-filled sky, the layer of fog settled over a forest of trees. His majesty and resplendency are in the way He shows us color—the oranges and yellows of fall leaves; the brilliant redness of a cardinal; the captivating hue of a bluebird; the pale, fresh green of leaves in the spring; a rainbow. All these give praise and glory to our Creator. His glory and majesty are manifest in all of creation.

Geographical Features

I am always reminded of God's glory and majesty in an American patriotic song I sang as a child in school. The lyrics of "America the Beautiful" give praise to the beauty of the sights, natural wonders, and landmarks of America.[1] America is described with its spacious skies, golden fields of grain, majestic mountains, and fruited plains. The song says that God has given His grace to America, something that always touched me as I grew to understand that these and other natural features in America are gifts given by God to bless us and show us His goodness, provision, and love. The images in the song celebrate the far-reaching majesty of God's creation in America, and for me they evoke feelings of pride in the country I'm blessed to live in and gratefulness to God for revealing His glory in this way.

America's national parks have some of the most majestic and beautiful visions I have ever seen:

- The Grand Canyon in Arizona, called one of the natural wonders of the world because of its immensity and spectacular rock formations, some of which feature colors that have taken millions of years to form

- Bryce Canyon in Utah, known for its spectacular spire-shaped rock formations

- Zion National Park, also in Utah, with its massive rock mountains, steep red cliffs, pools, waterfalls, and hanging gardens

- The Painted Desert in New Mexico, an incredible expanse of badland hills with glorious, rainbow-like colors

- The Grand Tetons in Wyoming and Glacier National Park in Montana, with their breathtaking snow-capped peaks

- California's Yosemite National Park, with its towering domed peaks, giant waterfalls, and high-country meadows

- The National Redwood Forest, also in California, with its enormous ancient trees

- Yellowstone National Park in Wyoming, known for Old Faithful and other geysers, magnificent waterfalls, hot springs, mud volcano, and amazing wildlife

- The great Alaskan wilderness, with gigantic glaciers, misty fjords, and the northern lights

- Niagara Falls in New York, bordering beautiful Canada, with its famous waterfalls, deemed one of the natural wonders of the world

- Haleakalā Crater in Hawaii and its amazing panoramic view, particularly at sunrise

- Also in Hawaii, the waterfalls of Hana's jungles and the active lava flows and steaming earth of Volcano National Park

These are only a few examples of His spectacular works of art in America, all of which bear witness to God's glory. But He made the entire world, and it's awe-inspiring to think of His glory and majesty manifest in nature all over the world. From Victoria Falls in Zambia and Zimbabwe to Mount Everest in the Himalayas, the Great Barrier Reef in Australia to Parícutin in Mexico, the Amazon rainforests in South America to Table Mountain in South Africa, Harbor of Rio de Janeiro in Brazil to the Puerto Princesa Underground River in the Philippines, God's creation is humbling, heart stopping, and miraculous, something no one else in the universe is capable of bringing about.

Natural Resources

God has given us the earth as a home, and He gave us natural resources in order to bless us and make our lives better. In so doing, He provided us with essential resources like land, water, and air but also oil, natural gas, coal, minerals, heavy metals, and more. We use these resources to survive and function in our daily lives, for instance, heating our homes or cooking with natural gas or fuel oil. Consider a few of these other resources and their uses:

- Iron ore is used in the construction of cars and buildings.
- Copper is used in electronics, as currency, and for jewelry.
- Quartz is used to make glass, watches, concrete, and silicon semiconductors.
- Calcium is used in foods, pharmaceuticals, cosmetics, plastics, and adhesives.
- Aluminum is used to build cars and planes and also in the bottling and canning industries.
- Petroleum is used to make clothing, ink, shampoo, bandages, heart valves, and nylon rope.
- Iodine is used in soaps, in cleaning products, and as an antiseptic.
- Barium is used in rubber, fireworks, X-ray technology, paint, and paper.
- Sulfur is used in wine making or for fruit preservation.
- Graphite is used in pencils and in brake linings.

To me, God's ability to create resources with all their varying chemical and physical properties attests to His goodness and glory. Only a marvelous God would do this for us.

We have also been given resources to enjoy. Precious metals, especially gold, silver, or copper; colored gemstones; sparkling white diamonds; and pearls are beautiful resources that display God's glory and point to His majesty. They're used in jewelry, as currency, or in art, but we also enjoy them for their practical uses. Gold, one of the most precious metals, is used in dentistry, medicine, computer circuitry, and scientific instruments. Silver is used in photography, electroplated wire, electronics, and chemistry.

God created an abundance of resources for our use. When God created people, He told us in Genesis 1:28, "Be fruitful and increase in number; fill the earth and subdue it. Rule over the fish in the sea and the birds in the sky and over every living creature that moves on the ground," and Genesis 2:15 says, "The Lord God took the man and put him in the Garden of Eden to work it and take care of it." I believe we need to be good stewards of the way we use the earth and the resources God gave us.

The Bible helps us to understand that the world is good. Though many Christians believe we live in a fallen world (after the original sin described in Genesis), which is no longer pure and uncorrupted, God's goodness was built into creation from the very beginning. Genesis 1:31 says, "God saw all that he had made, and it was very good." Psalm 136:1 says we should "Give thanks to the Lord, for he is good." Because God Himself is good and He declared that creation is good, it's important that we honor His provision of natural resources. I believe we can help preserve nonrenewable resources in the world by being conscious that these things are a gift, using them well, and using only what we need. Our consumption of natural resources makes an impact on the world God created and in the ability of people to flourish. If we think of the world as God's realm, we'll take our use of the resources in it more seriously, knowing we're accountable for how we live in it. And appreciating the glory and majesty of God through our consumption is one way to honor Him.

Our Design

As part of His creation, we also display God's glory and majesty in us. Human beings, as we discussed earlier, are marvelous and intricate creations. I believe we can experience and exhibit His goodness and glory through our design.

Take our senses, for example. Our interaction with and enjoyment of God's natural world can draw attention to His glory and majesty. When we engage our sense of smell, breathing in the fragrance after a rain, the scent of a flower, the aroma of a pine forest, the odor of freshly tilled soil, we can give praise to God's glory in a visceral way. When we delight in the color of the sky, are in awe of a nighttime moonbow, are inspired by a billowing white cloud, feel excitement about an approaching storm, marvel at a lightning-lit sky, or find peace in the quiet beauty of a misty morning, we show appreciation for God's majesty. When we respond emotionally to *any* of His natural creation, we are responding to His glory and majesty.

His glory comes through also in our facial expressions, a welcoming smile, a warm embrace, a gentle touch, a firm conviction, a person's laugh . . . in any situation. Genesis 1:27 reads, "So God created mankind in his own image, in the image of God he created them; male and female he created them." If God is glorious and He made us in His likeness, as His created beings, we display signs of His glory. We have His signature on us.

His glory and majesty are also seen in the talents that He's given us, and I believe He's given these to us in order to bring Him glory and praise. Some people are famous for living out their talents: Michelangelo for painting the ceiling of the Sistine Chapel and creating the *Pietà*; Leonardo da Vinci for painting *The Last Supper*; George Frideric Handel for composing the *Messiah*; Beethoven for composing *Symphony No. 9*; Giuseppe Verdi for composing *Requiem*; Itzhak Perlman, Van Cliburn, Isaac Stern, Jascha Heifetz, Yo-Yo Ma, and Vladimir Horowitz for being premier world-class musicians; Charlotte Church, Marilyn Horne, Joan Sutherland, and Luciano Pavarotti for performing with singing voices that stir the soul. Countless artists paint, construct, compose, play, sing, design, or build in ways that highlight God's glory and majesty. But I believe each one of us has been given a unique set of talents through which we, too, can glorify God. Whether through writing, cooking, teaching, programming, being an athlete, or anything else, we live out who we're created to be when we use our talents.

I will never forget once hearing opera singer, Kathleen Battle, perform at Atlanta Symphony Hall. For her encore, she sang simply, "If there is music in the air, there must be a God out there," which is a variation on an old Gospel song. The lyrics could not have expressed the idea of God's glory and majesty any more simply and poignantly. I think this is what living out our talents looks like. When we express ourselves through our talents, we exhibit something we've been given; this is our "music," and it points to God. This is a display of God's goodness and glory in us at the same time that it illuminates His own goodness and glory.

Whether we believe in God or not, His glory and majesty have been built into us and our sensibilities. In fact, they've been built into all of creation, including nature, geography, natural resources, even our interaction with these things. God speaks to us through His creation because He wants to bless us but also because He can only be who He is. Everything He made and touches displays His glory and majesty.

Revelation 19:6–7 says, "Hallelujah! For our Lord God Almighty reigns. Let us rejoice and be glad and give Him glory!" And Revelation 5:13 reads, "Then I heard every creature in heaven and on earth and under the earth and on the sea, and all that is in them, saying: 'To Him who sits on the throne and to the Lamb be praise and honor and glory and power, for ever and ever!'" All of creation and everything in it shows us that there's no one like Him.

I Am One, with You Forever

I open my heart, and it is filled with joy
to see the golden blaze in azure blue,
the glisten of dawn's first morning dew.
To hear the song-filled air of little birds,
such delight—a wonder to be heard.
To feel the warm breath of wind against my face,
the new season's gentle embrace.
To touch the sparkling velvet of the sand,
in cool waters where I stand.
This beauty is mine to behold,
my life it does truly mold.
Through nature I see God.
Revealed is The Path that I must trod.
The moment is eternity.
For somewhere is a sunset I must see,
God's eternal beauty enticing me.
My soul is now at peace and rest
for I am one with You at last, at last.

—Rhonda Dawes Milner

CHAPTER 7

God's Miracles
and Creativity

He is the one you praise; he is your God, who per-
formed for you those great and awesome won-
ders you saw with your own eyes.

DEUTERONOMY 10:21

THE BIBLE TELLS US THAT JESUS PERFORMED MIRACLES.
He healed the blind. He calmed storms. He walked on water. He turned
water into wine. He fed thousands of people with only five loaves of
bread and two small fish. I believe He did this because He genuinely
cared about people and wanted to help them.

At the same time, His miracles revealed something about the authen-
ticity of God. When Jesus performed miracles, people took notice and
thought about who He was and what He was capable of. His miracles
pointed *to* God.

God's miracles are still all around us today, evident in big, powerful,
life-changing ways and also observable in simple, meaningful, quiet ways.
He performs these supernatural acts for the same reason: to touch and

transform our lives and to show us He is the God of the universe. We can find His miracles in nature, the characteristics and behaviors of animals, and in our own human bodies. Though I've touched on many examples of God's signature in His creation in previous chapters, I'd like to further illustrate how He blesses us through the miracles of His creation because I think they help us learn something about God's heart, creativity, and authority. Even more, I believe that God's miracles in creation offer us some fascinating metaphors for faith and truths about life.

John 2:11 says, "What Jesus did here in Cana of Galilee was the first of the signs through which he revealed his glory; and his disciples believed in him." God sometimes performs miracles, building amazing details into nature, living beings, and the circumstances of our existence, so we might believe in Him. I think that when we open our eyes to these details, we can see how He desires to reach us through them.

Miracles in the Natural World

God interacts with His creation through miracles in nature. They are intentional displays of His participation in our lives in extraordinary ways. I highlight them because they teach us lessons about ourselves, God, and life, and yet we often miss them or minimize their significance.

Think about how a pearl is created, for example. It starts out as a tiny piece of sand or grit that has gained entrance into an oyster shell. Because the foreign substance is an irritant to the oyster inside the shell, the oyster covers it with layers and layers of a natural substance—mother-of-pearl—until the piece of sand or grit is coated in hundreds of layers. I find it amazing that this process starts with nothing except a piece of sand or grit and ends up as a beautiful, opalescent pearl. In a similar way, this miracle in nature points to the faith journey we have as people. We are like the little piece of sand or grit, something seemingly ordinary or insignificant, until God covers us spiritually with Christ to make us pure and, as it says in Isaiah 1:18, "white as snow" in the darkness of our sins and imperfections. As God demonstrated through His creation of the pearl, He can turn us into something wonderful and beautiful, continually covering and refining us to make us into the people that He always meant for us to be.

In a similar way, we are also like gemstones that start out as mere rocks in the earth but then are refined and polished by God until they become jewels. He brings us as people through refining experiences and polishes us with His care, helping us to know Jesus. As He does this, when we come to faith, we become something new and beautiful, the precious jewels He always knew we were.

Geodes offer a metaphor for life as well. On the outside, they look like regular rocks, plain and nondescript. But if you crack them open, inside you find beautiful, sparkling crystals. In 1 Samuel 16:7, God says, "The Lord does not look at the things people look at. People look at the outward appearance, but the Lord looks at the heart." The geode is a reminder to us that it's not the outside of a person that is the most important but who they are on the inside that counts. The character of a person is the most precious and beautiful part of who they are.

The metaphors we find through God's creation extend to the plant world. Think of the way a growing bush needs to be pruned back occasionally in order to strengthen the whole plant and support new growth. The pruning itself can be deep and brutal, but it produces new fruit and causes the plant to flourish. It's interesting that God would design things to work like this. Yet, this process resonates with us in our experience as people who are also God's creation. At times we may experience pain or hardship. These are part of living in a fallen world. But He has every compassion for us in these moments of life and in fact uses these experiences to get our attention, help us figure out what's most important, or develop spiritually and emotionally. Though heartache and suffering are hard, He knows we can grow stronger, wiser, kinder, and more faithful through them, which allows us to become who we were meant to be. In addition, God tells us in Hebrews 13:5, "Never will I leave you; never will I forsake you." He promises to never abandon us in our pain, saying instead that He will walk with us and help us in every moment of our human suffering.

There are other examples of God's miracles and creativity in the plant kingdom. Why do some flowers close at night, while others do not? How do flowers create their beautiful fragrance, allowing them to attract bees and aid in their own pollination? How does a small acorn grow to become a magnificent tree? When you observe the beauty and marvel of plants, trees, or flowers in and of themselves, they are complete miracles. Even if we, as humans, had the ability to create a beautiful, wondrous, well-thought-out plant, we wouldn't have the ability to create the hundreds of thousands of other plants, trees, or flowers that exist on our planet, let alone the creatures and ecosystems that exist around them. What about the fruits, nuts, vegetables, and grains that come from these, providing us with the sustenance and nutrients we and other creatures need to survive? Or think about photosynthesis, with its by-product of oxygen and ability to produce breathable air; it's a miraculous system, created to benefit all of creation. These systems work for our benefit. God's creativity along with His countless miracles provide such loving care for us, His children.

Miracles in the Animal Kingdom

The creatures God made to inhabit the earth with us also have amazing characteristics. We can observe the behaviors and processes of these creatures because He's placed His creation around us to remind us of who He is. Their design is at once inventive, original, and miraculous, pointing to the reality of their Creator.

Think of the miracle of an egg. God created a self-contained world in an egg, an environment outside of the mother's body for a bird, reptile, or other creature to develop in. The parent must keep the egg safe and warm in order for it to hatch, but something else must stimulate the development of the creature inside the egg. And something else must provide the energy that's needed to trigger the cell division. The beginning of life and transformation from cell to newborn creature point to the work of God.

Think also of the amazing and inexplicable phenomenon of bird migration. Birds have the strength to fly thousands of miles, some across deserts or huge bodies of water, others even traveling twice across the entire hemisphere and back. How do they make these incredible journeys, and what kind of sophisticated internal navigation systems allow them to do this? How is it possible that millions of birds from across different climates and areas know to time their migration so precisely? How do they coordinate and fly in such perfect formation? And how do they implicitly know where to go and how to return to the same place every year? Yet millions of birds, some weighing less than an ounce, do this instinctively and with an enormous amount of energy. Their migration is crucial to their survival, beautiful to witness, and both a mystery and miracle of God.

And what about the migration of whales? How salmon know to swim upstream in order to give birth and die? Why Canada geese mate for life, never taking another mate, even if their mate is lost? How does a newborn marsupial know it must climb up to find its mother's pouch in order to survive? What makes it possible for a hummingbird to move its wings so fast that the wings are barely visible? So many unanswerable quandaries and miracles in nature can only point to the existence of a Creator. Miracles in nature are real.

Metamorphosis as a Metaphor

I believe miracles in the animal kingdom also offer interesting metaphors for faith and life. You may have learned about the life cycle of a butterfly or moth at some point during your school career. A caterpillar hatches from an egg as a larva, and during its first stage of life, it eats all day long because it needs to consume enough food to be able to enter its pupal stage, undergo a complete metamorphosis inside its chrysalis, and have enough energy to emerge as an adult butterfly. Shortly before its metamorphosis, it enters a pupa (often referred to as a cocoon) that is so tightly woven that the caterpillar's air supply is cut off, it loses its ability to move, and it is no longer able to eat. For the caterpillar, God specifically chose to make this the process for metamorphosis.

Inside the pupa, the caterpillar's body becomes like a corpse of sorts. It releases enzymes that cause much of its body to dissolve before the remaining tissues and cells produce new body parts, allowing it to become a butterfly. Before this full cycle can be complete, the butterfly first has to emerge from the pupa in order to survive. To do this, the encased butterfly begins to move and stretch its wings, pushing against the inside of the pupa. As it meets resistance, it pushes harder, a process God designed so that its wings could develop and the butterfly could gain the strength it needs to thrive outside of the pupa. When it finally emerges, it not only looks different but also has the ability to fly. It is new, transformed, and beautiful.

This fascinating occurrence in nature is a miracle. But why must it undergo such a rigorous and laborious process of emersion? Some evolutionary theory asserts that nature, on its own, drifts toward simplicity rather than complexity. But the butterfly's metamorphosis does not conserve energy and doesn't seem to be consistent with this kind of evolutionary theory. I believe the process—in fact, the entire life cycle of a butterfly—points to the existence of a Creator.

Among other things, I believe God also uses the caterpillar to communicate a love story to us about the miracle of renewal. Jesus, when He allowed Himself to be punished and crucified to take on all the sins and wrongdoing of humankind, willingly entered a time of hardship and suffering that put Him in the most physically humble, emotionally vulnerable, and spiritually destitute situation in history. This was the only way life, spiritual rebirth, and salvation could happen.

As the caterpillar gives us its body, Jesus gives up His life for humankind. In historical accounts of Jesus's death and resurrection, His body is wrapped in a white shroud, and strips of cloth securely bind Him, a similar image to the caterpillar being tightly bound and enshrouded in its pupa. Jesus's body is placed in a dark cave, its entrance sealed by a large stone. He is in the dark, without fresh air, without food, unable to move. When, through the power of God, He emerges alive from His tomb, everything is different. He emerges as glorious, and His resurrection allows the fate of mankind to forever be changed. The new, resurrected Jesus will, at the right time, ascend into Heaven to sit at the right hand of God, the Father. He will be released from the life lived on earth. Peter, one of Jesus's disciples, is not there to see Jesus emerge from the tomb, but he finds Jesus's shroud still bound, evidence that Jesus is alive in spite of the fact that others had seen His dead body. I've told you this story to illustrate that the process of transformation in a caterpillar is a direct metaphor for Jesus's death and resurrection. God wrote His signature into the life cycle of a caterpillar.

Because of Jesus's resurrection, we can choose to have faith in Him, enter a state of transformation in our lives when we believe in His sovereignty and grace, and emerge as if reborn, a new creation. This is spiritual rebirth. It happens in our hearts and souls. We cannot change without giving up our old ways and our old lives. And when we choose to trust and believe in Jesus, we become our true selves, who God always created us to be, and we are beautiful. God promises not only a new life but also eternity with Him in Heaven. To me, all this is once again what the metamorphosis of a caterpillar can remind us of. If we simply look at God's creation, we can see how He communicates His love and existence to us.

In a similar way, we can observe the lives and behaviors of other creatures to learn some metaphorical truths. Dragonflies, for example, may cause us to reflect on what happens after we pass away but live on in Christ. Author Doris Stickney wrote a book for children called *Water Bugs and Dragonflies* to help them understand death.[1] In it, a water bug lives only in the water until one day it climbs up on a reed and experiences a change in its body, growing wings and a long tail. It has become a dragonfly, now able to take to the air, but at the same time, it realizes that it can never go back to live underwater. It can see the other water bugs below, but it cannot communicate with them. I find this to be a powerful metaphor for life, death, and eternal life. When we have faith in Jesus, the life of a dragonfly can reassure us that we are transformed into a new form after we die. Like the dragonfly in the story, we can see our loved ones, wishing them great care and love from our current state, but we cannot communicate with them. God makes it so that even as we are absent from our old body, we can be present with Him in eternity because He has made us alive through Jesus's sacrifice. When we believe in Him, this is our reality. I find it poignant that even the life of a small dragonfly can give us a glimpse or reminder of God's care and salvation.

And there are even more transformations in nature that point to Him, each one its own miracle:

- Frogs change significantly during their life cycles. Tadpoles develop into frogs, becoming something completely different from what they were before. Initially, they were only aquatic creatures, but in their new state, they become amphibious, able to now walk on land.

- Maggots, at first worm-like in feature, enter a pupa stage and emerge as flies. They are completely different in appearance and are now able to fly.

- Ladybugs start out as small, black, worm-like larvae. After their yellow pupa stage, they appear as the red insects with black spots that we recognize.

Why is there metamorphosis in nature? Again, from a scientific or evolutionary standpoint, metamorphosis is not an efficient or a logical process. It doesn't conserve energy at the same time that it is bringing something to a higher state, and it adds complexity to a transformation that should otherwise be more simplistic. But I believe metamorphosis is possible and present by our Creator's design. It communicates the story He has planned for us and particularly His ultimate story of love for us in Jesus, His Son. None of the creatures mentioned in this section appear as they did before. God wrote them into nature to remind us of who He is, show us truths about change, and help us see that when we believe in Him, we are ourselves a new creation.

Miracles in the Human Body

The human body is the most amazing display of God's creation and miraculous creativity. The way it works far surpasses anything that even the most finely tuned of machines could achieve. We move and function and exist as if automatically. Yet in so many ways, the parts and systems of our bodies—in fact, all the things that make us human—remain largely unexplainable.

Our Hearts

The heart, which maintains life, is itself a miracle. This muscle acts as a pump to circulate our blood into our lungs for oxygenation and then the oxygenated blood through our body to all our organs. From the time it begins to beat in utero at around three weeks gestational age to when our body fails to function at death, it never stops—not for a single moment of rest. How does it never fatigue or rest in our lifetime? The ability of the heart to function is not something that might, in other situations, seem logical or possible to us, but God works the miracle in it. Somehow, in an unexplainable way, this is what He makes possible with the heart.

We know that the heart begins to beat at 22 days after conception, but what starts it? Does it start to beat spontaneously on its own? As with other systems in the natural world, energy is needed in order for anything to start, but where does this energy come from? From the first division of the zygote—the cell that develops into a human being—the heart is already alive and growing. It is the first organ to get everything going and is absolutely required for life. The fact that the heart begins like this and not long after it starts to beat is a miracle of life.

Our Thoughts

Our neurological system is the source of our thoughts. We cannot see or touch our thoughts, they appear to have no physical substance to them, and yet they are real. When do thoughts start in our conscious mind? What causes them? How do we produce them? Once the process starts, it never stops. If you were to try to void your mind of thoughts, thinking absolutely nothing, you would still be thinking something. You could try, to a certain extent, to meditate, focusing on your breathing or a repeated word, but you would still be thinking. And even if you could control things so that you have just one thought, you'd still be thinking. Sooner or later, your mind would involuntarily go to the next thought. Even during sleep, your brain dreams and processes thoughts. Scientists have studied neurotransmitters and the emotions or feelings they contribute to, areas of brains and neurological pathways, and neural functioning. But no one has been able to explain the process of thinking, how it happens, and why we never stop doing it. It's a mystery and a miracle.

Our Growth

Human and embryonic development is also a mystery. It all begins with two gametes, the sperm and the egg, which combine to form the fertilized ovum or zygote that each of us begins from. Does the energy for this come from the tiny, propelled sperm? What triggers the massive duplication of the cells to form a human being? How do the cells divide and become specialized to turn into certain parts of the body? Doctors and scientists have uncovered so much, yet they still can't explain the *whys* of the beginning of life. When you consider the embryology of humans, such complexity is truly mind-boggling.

Humans have a specific number of germ cells that contain all the genetic information from our ancestors. This information is transmitted from generation to generation through our germ cells. Miraculously, they contain all the genetic coding needed to produce life. We each have twenty-three pairs of chromosomes, twenty-two creating our phenotype and the twenty-third determining our sexual makeup. These chromosomes are composed of DNA as a double helix. Our sex cells, or gametes, the sperm and egg, each have one half of the double helix, which at conception joins together with the other to produce the fertilized ovum. The ovum then rapidly divides to produce an embryo, which has the capacity to grow into a fetus, then neonate, baby, toddler, child, adolescent, teenager, young adult, and mature adult. It's amazing that we have the capacity to grow and develop like this.

As part of the amazing process for creating life, God offers another metaphor through which we may comprehend His love. When the closest and most physically intimate relationship we can have with someone is expressed through intercourse, two people become one, joining in a union. This is a metaphor of God's love for us. He desires to be close to us in heart and spirit, to have a deep and meaningful intimacy with us. This is a divine communion in which we, within our spiritual beings, join with God for eternity. The loving relationship we have with our spouse in our lifetime on earth is just a glimmer of the loving relationship we'll have with God in our life in eternity, after we pass away. Because we're made by Him in His image, He has built in us the desire to be in relationship with Him and others. So the blessing of loving one another on earth is a beautiful way through which He grows us in faith and love. And how creative and miraculous that out of this reality, God also brings about the conception of a baby for new life.

From the metaphor of God's love for us in conception springs another beautiful metaphor, this one about the transformation of our lives from birth to eternal life. As a growing embryo and then fetus in the womb, a baby is in a safe, secure, warm, and peaceful environment. The baby is fed, and everything is provided for him or her. I marvel that a woman's body has the ability to expand, nurture the growth and development of a human being, and deliver this human being into the world. At a certain point, the placenta begins to deteriorate as its blood supply from the mother atrophies and the baby becomes too big for the environment in the womb. So labor is stimulated. During delivery, physical stimulation through the birth canal enables the newborn's respiratory system to function, and because of this, the newborn takes its first breath and becomes alive in the outside world.

This is a painful process of being forced from a safe and familiar environment to one of harsh lights, cold air, and unfamiliarity. The baby is suddenly no longer connected to his or her mother and may feel vulnerable, afraid, or alone. No wonder babies cry out at birth. But in crying, the baby is prompted to breathe, which forces air into their lungs. Then, medically speaking, prostaglandins are released, stimulating the closure of the ductus arteriosus part of embryonic circulation; as this happens, the baby is becoming something new and different from what he or she was in the environment of their mother's uterus.

As we grow from childhood into adulthood, our biological systems mature first, and our brains reach full maturity in our midtwenties. Whereas we had initially wanted to cling to our world inside the womb as babies, we now find other environments we may enjoy more. Eventually something happens on the cellular level that triggers senescence, or the process of becoming old. Our cells begin aging or deteriorating, progressing in this way over time until our bodies can no longer function properly, we reach old age, and we pass away.

Interestingly, up until the point of death, we have energy—our heart beats, our brain thinks, our body systems continue to function. As I mentioned earlier in the book, scientists have determined that energy cannot be created or destroyed. So when a person passes away, where does the life energy of that person go? I believe there's much more to us than tissues and cells. There's something spiritual and eternal built into us that makes us who we are for eternity; the energy in us goes beyond our time on earth, and to me, this is completely miraculous. We are miracles of God.

In a spiritual and metaphorical sense, just as the womb prepares us for our life on earth, our life on earth prepares us for our eternal life. We exist on earth to develop our souls, minds, hearts, and spirits—our eternal organs—to be able to enter into eternity with God. Just as we leave the womb, we one day leave the temporal world to discover a new eternal world with God. Just as we'd clung so powerfully to the womb, not knowing what the world held for us, we often cling to the world we live in, not realizing that a whole other world exists outside of ours, and God has always meant for us to be there with Him one day. Just as the conditions during labor and delivery prepare us and make us stronger for the world, the difficult conditions in our lives now can serve to prepare us and make us stronger, more ready to transition to our life in eternity with God at the right time. And even though death and grief are hard and real, beyond this present life is a much bigger and richer life to experience.

This is what growth in a human being can look like. The way our bodies physically grow and develop throughout the course of our lives is nothing short of miraculous. But the way we grow and develop spiritually, knowing that we're made for a world beyond this one, is literally life changing.

The creativity in how God communicates His love for us through creation has no limits. Whether through His miracles in the natural world, animal kingdom, or our own human bodies, He is absolutely amazing. He reaches out to us through not only scientific knowledge and understanding but also signs and metaphors He's built into His creation. I'm grateful for His design, His goodness, and His faithfulness to us.

Snowflakes

Still and quiet, I want your peace.
Miracle crystals each one unique.
You mold together to all form
smooth white blankets all the norm.
Each flake has no conformity
just like humans with no uniformity.
A microcosm of our humanity—
If we look, we will see.
Ever present everywhere
then you vanish into thin air.
When I gaze into nature,
I see God.
Tiny snowflakes He made so fair.
Where do we go, oh where, oh where?

—Rhonda Dawes Milner

Part 2

God's Signature
in Our Lives

CHAPTER 8

God's Mystery
and Omniscience

"For my thoughts are not your thoughts, neither are
your ways my ways," declares the Lord. "As the heavens
are higher than the earth, so are my ways higher than
your ways and my thoughts than your thoughts."

ISAIAH 55:8–9

THERE IS MUCH MYSTERY TO GOD IN THAT THERE ARE so many things that we do not understand on this earth, things we will not be able to understand until we are one day in His glorious presence. We can learn, study, and experience many things in our lifetime. But as created beings rather than the Creator, we are limited in our ability to know it all. What is reassuring is that God, as we established earlier in the book, is omniscient. He possesses complete awareness and understanding of all things, and He knows and sees the big picture of His plan. To that end, He is gracious to shape the circumstances of our lives so that we can have hope and trust in Him, ultimately living out the lives He created us for, knowing who He is, and having a close and personal relationship with Him. Among other things, He signs His name in all of creation, including the situations in our lives, to help us see and believe in Him.

God knows where He's put us in life and why things happen. His signature is in our everyday circumstances, and we can count on the fact that He has our best interests at heart. Though we may not always know the outcome of a situation, the Bible tells us that we can rely on Him. In 1 Timothy 3:16 we read, "Beyond all question, the mystery from which true godliness springs is great." Deuteronomy 29:29 tells us, "The secret things belong to the Lord our God, but the things revealed belong to us and to our children forever, that we may follow all the words of this law." God's reasoning may be mysterious to us at times, but we can trust in His omniscience and goodness.

I believe God's signature in the world carries certain implications for us. As we witness the many signs He has put in creation and consider the circumstances in which He's placed us, we're called to some kind of response. When He's placed the truths of who He is and the way He works before us, we find ourselves at a bit of a crossroad. We can either choose to lean toward Him in faith, taking a step forward in belief, or we can choose to lean away from Him, downplaying what we've seen. In either scenario, He loves us incredibly; but the life He has always meant for us is one in which we recognize our Creator, know that He's made us special, always feel close to Him, and live a life of purpose and meaning in Him.

God's Understanding of
Our Circumstances

God guides and directs all the experiences and circumstances of our lives. He shapes every situation for our good and so we can know the assurance of His love. But why is the world full of darkness, hurt, and maliciousness if God is loving and all powerful? Why do horrible things happen to good people if God is so good? And how should we respond when we find ourselves in painful situations? I believe we start by knowing that God loves us. In 1 John 4:19, the Bible tells us, "We love because he first loved us." When we have assurance of God's love, we are bolstered by it and, with His help, have greater capacity to love in return. We can love Him, love others, and love through situations more.

God created us to be in relationship with Him yet gave us the choice and free will to decide whether we would ourselves choose to follow Him. I believe He did this because we weren't designed to be puppets. Love cannot exist unless there is free choice, and real love and devotion means that we make a decision to follow Him. A person can't force another person to love them, nor would that person feel truly valued if someone just loved them because they had no other choice.

God always loves us, but when we choose to love Him back, a beautiful and sometimes supernatural thing happens. Through the help of His Spirit, we gain greater insight and a desire to try to bring out the best in a situation. With free choice, we can try to make something good come out of something bad, and I think that is what God wants us to do.

We're also able to do this because we believe, in the big scheme of things, that God knows exactly what He's doing. Again, I want to draw your attention to Romans 8:28 where it says, "And we know that in all things God works for the good of those who love him, who have been called according to his purpose." God engineers the circumstances of our lives out of His care and loving-kindness and shapes every situation for our good. As an omniscient God, nothing is a surprise to Him, and He can use it to grow us closer to Him and bless the world around us. I also think that we see God's will for our life by what happens to us and how we respond to it.

I know stories of how incredible people have taken tragedies in their lives and turned the final outcome into something good. I have friends who have started nonprofits to raise awareness and to make changes that may save other families from the heartbreak of losing a child or seeing loved ones suffer. My friends Steve and Susan Owings suffered a terrible loss when their older son was killed in an automobile crash in which a tractor-trailer, going over the speed limit, slammed into his car. His younger brother, who was also with him, survived the accident, and their older son died in his brother's arms. This is the kind of tragedy that most of us cannot and do not ever want to imagine, but the Owings family did an amazing thing: They used their tremendous grief and loss to found an organization called Road Safe America, which protects people from the dangerous conditions of big rigs and huge trucks. They turned their pain and heartache into something positive that would save people and make a difference in the world.

The Shepherd Center is a world-renowned spinal cord and brain injury rehabilitation center. It was founded by an amazing family I know who also suffered great tragedy in their lives. Harold and Alana Shepherd, along with their son James and other important individuals, created the Shepherd Center after James was injured in a bodysurfing accident that left him paralyzed from the neck down because of a serious spinal cord injury. At the time, there were no such facilities in the southeastern part of the United States. Recognizing a huge need, these groundbreaking individuals founded the hospital, which today is a huge state-of-the art facility that has improved countless lives and given hope to so many.

My friend Mary Jane Stafford founded Grateful Hearts Ministries to help women stuck in hard places in their lives. She did this in part because, through the painful experience of addiction she saw around her, God opened her eyes to the pain of other women caught in addiction. She allowed God to transform her heartache for those around her into something good and beautiful, and turned her efforts outward in order to impact women's lives. Today, the ministry she began helps to restore the lives of an untold number of women and families. Grateful Hearts Ministries is a nonprofit organization that helps and shares God's love with homeless, addicted, and incarcerated women. It's humbling and incredible to think how Mary Jane took a painful situation in her life and made it into something that changes lives and gives the glory to God for it. Through her willingness to show others the love of God, they, too, have the opportunity to know Him.

On any scale, you can take hardship and difficult situations and make a decision to respond in a way that honors God and impacts people around you. Years ago, I gave my husband two English Pointers as a birthday gift. These sweet dogs loved to run and would sometimes find ways to get loose from our house or yard. On one of these days, some neighbors called animal control, and our dogs were taken without our knowledge. For days we were unable to find them or to get the story of what had happened. Our inquiries were met with silence, signs we'd posted went unanswered, and the animal control center said it did not have our dogs. My heart told me to go to the animal control center anyway, but because it was the weekend by that point, I couldn't go in. I was there as soon as the doors first opened on Monday morning, but much to my chagrin, I discovered that our wonderful dogs had been euthanized that very morning. Our family was heartbroken.

As I slowly recovered from the shock of this tragedy, I began to question the situation. It was upsetting to realize that the animal control center in my area did not scan pets for microchips, only held animals for up to 72 hours, and was not readily open to the public so that families could search for their missing pets. If a pet were to run away and be picked up by animal control while a family was out of town, I realized it was highly possible, if not probable, that this pet could be euthanized before the family even learned their pet was lost. This injustice motivated me to take action.

Though I felt much sadness, I knew that God could bring good out of any situation. I decided to find a way to do something that would honor Him and make things better for others. I approached the press to raise awareness, went before commissioners to lobby for positive change in the management of the animal control facility, and rallied people in the community. Because of these efforts, inhumane policies were removed and the facility was even opened to the public for pet adoptions. A friend and I joined forces to do a fund-raiser for the facility and eventually founded a nonprofit organization called New Leash on Life in order to benefit, advocate for, and protect animals in our community.

What I never expected was that this experience of losing my dogs and creating a nonprofit was God's preparation to help me deal with and react to the worst tragedy of my life. Sometime later, I found myself again in a position of trying to choose to bring good from an awful loss—this time, the loss of my twenty-five-year-old son. In April 2011, on a beautiful spring day, my son had had friends over to our house to enjoy the pool after a day outing. He had been planning a trip to the Bahamas to spearfish and was using our swimming pool to practice breath-holding. He blacked out but no one noticed, because most of his friends had left for the evening. I discovered him the next evening when I returned from out of town. Unbeknownst to me at the time, he had died from something called shallow water blackout, a silent killer that even expert swimmers could succumb to after underwater breath-holding. It occurs when someone passes out before they have the urge to breathe. From this enormous heartache, I founded an organization called Shallow Water Blackout Prevention to raise awareness of and educate others about the risks and dangers of underwater breath-holding. My website www.shallowwaterblackoutprevention.org went live in June 2011.

I believe God wants us to choose good even when we have been knocked down or attacked by evil. He is loving, wise, and powerful and can bless and multiply our efforts in ways we might never imagine. If we love and trust in Him, we know that He will not allow difficult situations to conquer us. Through the mystery of His ways and because He is an omniscient God, He knows exactly how to make good come out of tragedy.

God's Understanding of Our Spirit

Delving a little more into the theology side of things, I think we are moved to trust in God when we realize how much He loves us. He knows everything about us—every single detail, thought, or feeling—and He loves us enough to have given up His whole life for us. There's not a tear we cry that He doesn't see. There's not a moment of our life that He isn't present for. There's not a thing we've done that's a surprise to Him. Psalm 139:1–4 tells us "You have searched me, Lord, and you know me. You know when I sit and when I rise; you perceive my thoughts from afar. You discern my going out and my lying down; you are familiar with all my ways. Before a word is on my tongue you, Lord, know it completely." There's not a thing He doesn't know, and there's not a God who loves us more.

Trusting Him allows us to choose good over evil, right from wrong, forgiveness over condemnation, patience over anger, peace over chaos. God knows how to help us in all the circumstances of our lives, and He does this because He knows our spirit. Søren Kierkegaard—philosopher, theologian, and writer—said that God created us to be in relationship with Him, others, and ourselves. At its core, our spirit is relational, and he believed that this component of spirit is innate in us. Because of this, he recognized that as human beings, we could never be fully understood in purely physical or scientific terms.[1] Our relationship with God is what allows us to become who He created us to be.

C. S. Lewis said much the same thing in *The Problem of Pain*, writing that our home is to be in relationship with God.[2] If all this is true, to trust in God and be in relationship with Him requires a surrender and loss of our old self—essentially, who we were and the way we did things before we became aware that He is God. When we accept God's will for our lives, we relinquish our will. This doesn't mean that we become brainwashed or spineless; but it does mean we are made new, inheriting our birthright and becoming our true selves because of our new identity in Christ. We relinquish our will because once we know He's the omniscient, all-powerful, omnipresent Creator of the universe and the God who loves us so much that He actually saves us from ourselves, we can't help but to realize His way is better.

To choose God and turn toward Him means that we're also turning away from something else. As I mentioned, we must give up the way we thought things were before. Conversely, when we choose something else over God, we separate ourselves from Him and turn away from His goodness. Does He still love us and show us His goodness? Yes. But anything that we choose to turn toward and rely on more than God falls short. God knows that in the end, we'll ultimately miss the purpose for which we were created. We also do Him a great dishonor.

This is what original sin looked like. The Bible tells us that God didn't make the Garden of Eden with evil in it. In fact, He made it to be amazing for Adam and Eve. But Satan, in turning away from God in Heaven, gave rise to evil, and when Adam and Eve listened to Satan in the Garden of Eden, they made a choice to turn away from God. Their actions brought sin to humankind and cursed the way the natural world works, and we've lived in a fallen state ever since.

Eve's desire to disobey God and gain knowledge for herself demonstrated prideful thinking, the idea that she knew what was better for her than God did. But the fall happened because of her distrust and desire to follow her own will over God's.[3] We don't always realize the ways in which we're prideful, thinking we know better than God does. But when we turn from God, we turn to sin. When we've been presented with the truth of who God is, *not* trusting Him is sin.

Kierkegaard calls sin the opposite of faith and says that for us, trusting in God ultimately becomes a "leap of faith" based on our free choice.[4] When we find out who God is, particularly as He speaks to us through

His Holy Spirit, through the circumstances of our lives and through all the signs He's left for us in creation, we can turn to Him, choosing to follow the destiny for which we were created.

There will always be a tension on this side of Heaven that's tied to belief. It's like there are two seeds in us, one from Adam and one from God—one from the flesh and one from the Spirit—both competing for our life. We can choose God or not; we can accept God's will or we can refuse to relinquish our own will. Whichever seed we choose to water and nourish will be the one that grows. Because both seeds are part of who we are, they are always present in us, each one prepared to grow. We need to choose which seed to water daily and which one to commit and recommit to. As humans who are made out of both flesh and spirit, this is the dualism in us.

God created us to be in spirit and relationship with Him. This doesn't mean we will be without sin in our lives. Again, we live in a fallen world. We sometimes choose ourselves over God and then feel the consequences and ripple effects of that. And there is sin in the world around us as a result of the fall and sin in other people. Things are not perfect. In fact, they can be pretty bad. But when we trust and follow God, we can choose Him, and in so doing, we are choosing against evil.

Theodicy is the study of God's love and goodness in the world in light of the evil that nonetheless exists. It's one of the conditions in the world that's sometimes hard to understand. Evil will happen. Plenty of people choose against God. But when we believe in God, we can choose to not let evil defeat us. We can choose right over wrong, kindness over selfishness, grace over unforgiveness. We've been given free will, and with it, we can freely choose, again and again, good over evil. We have the ability to not let evil defeat us but instead can, with God's help, transform a situation. During a tragic occurrence, we can choose to be God's vessel for good and to give God our trust.

Living in a fallen world means we witness effects of the Holocaust, 9/11, Hurricane Katrina, an earthquake in Haiti, or an international health epidemic. Satan also brings evil into the natural world itself. Only God can understand why there is needless, painful, and unexplainable suffering in people's lives and how He can help and restore them. He knows that all ends well in the end, and He has every compassion for us. We can only see things from a limited human perspective during our time on earth. As with a needlepoint tapestry, the needlepoint looks like a disorganized mess of random colors and threads from below, but from above—God's perspective—it is a beautiful design and makes sense. God, in His omniscience, knows all the reasons for troubles in this life because He sees the big picture that we, in our mortal bodies, cannot.

When we suffer or grieve in life, God uses our pain and brokenness to help us grow and become the people that He created us to be. I mentioned in an earlier chapter that a butterfly, when it's ready to emerge from its cocoon, needs to struggle to break free. The struggle strengthens its wings so that it can fly and survive. Our own struggles in life, as painful and insurmountable as they may be, can help us grow stronger and develop a strength and character we might not otherwise be able to develop if we don't meet that adversity. Then, as we grow and develop spiritually and emotionally, we become the people we're meant to be.

Similarly, life encompasses both mountains and valleys. Each one is necessary in order to have the other. We wouldn't be able to fully appreciate the joys of the high places in our lives without the sorrow of the low places. A friend of mine once wisely pointed out that mountaintops are not where we typically experience all our personal and spiritual growth, as mountaintops above the tree line are barren. But in the deep valleys of pain and suffering are where we grow and change, as valleys are often green, lush, and full of growth.

When we choose to trust in God and follow His ways, the outcome of a situation and the outcome of our lives are completely changed. He knows us and designed us to be in relationship with Him, and to that end He's put everything before us to help us have faith in Him. Probably the biggest testimony to God's existence and His love for us is in how people's lives become transformed when they believe in Jesus. People can seldom truly change unless they have been transformed by the power of the Holy Spirit in Christ.

I'm so grateful for the way He's signed His name on me and all the circumstances of my life. I don't profess to know His reasoning for everything—He is a God of wonder and mystery, and I am His creation—but I also recognize that He is good, and if I had all the answers, I would look only to myself instead of to Him. As a human being, I can never hope to know Him fully or understand His mind. But I know He works all things for my good, and I believe He's called me to His purpose. I've taken a leap of faith, and I trust Him.

When You Don't Understand

When life makes no sense and you don't understand
the reason why
Your life unravels before your very eyes

You look to find an answer somewhere
You look to find something, someone to help and care

Your heart is crushed, torn, and broken
So many words have been left unspoken

The tears roll out from a hidden, deep place
The hurt and heartbreak show all over your face

Life seems unbearable with shame and disgrace
You look to find shelter, but there is no place

The hurt is too much to try to carry on
Your heartstrings are cut, losing their song

Is it possible to still make your way?
Can you go on breathing for another day?

You think your heart will stop, will miss its next beat
The dark specter lurks near, waiting to leap

Cold, still sleep seems to be the only answer
Fear and sadness have become your cancer

You question if you are going insane
You don't know how to play this heart game

There is nowhere left to go
Never have you felt so very, very low

You don't understand the reason or cause for such hurt
You wish there was someone to help and alert

The sadness looms and does not go away
Speaking is useless, there is nothing left to say

When the cruel words are like a viper's sting
The pain still echoes with a continuous ring

You feel like a broken and wounded bird
You only want your hurt and sorrow to be
acknowledged and heard

Who is there to turn to, but only God
But only stillness and silence, there is no nod

Sometimes no response can give you grace
Unanswered prayers may be the case

You scream and cry out with all your might
Please dear God help make things right

You won't give in, give up the fight
Your faith in Him will never lose its sight

In unexplained mystery you must rest
God's help and His strength are still your quest

He will be found because you seek
Blessed are the suffering, not just the meek

You will continue your trust and your belief
Even if Heaven will be your only relief

Your faith in God alone, you will always keep
What is sown on earth, in Heaven you will reap

—*Rhonda Dawes Milner*

CHAPTER 9

God's Truth and Wisdom

*Trust in the Lord with all your heart and lean not
on your own understanding; in all your ways sub-
mit to him, and he will make your paths straight.*

PROVERBS 3:5–6

GOD IS THE SOURCE AND EMBODIMENT OF ALL TRUTH.
He wants us to be able to know the truth and to have our lives better
because of it. So He reveals it to us through the person of Jesus, in what
the Bible says about Him, and in how the Holy Spirit convicts us of Him.
In Him we know what is real and good and right in life; and from Him
comes all wisdom.

Jesus tells us in John 14:6, "I am the way and the truth and the life.
No one comes to the Father except through me." In John 18:37 He says,
"The reason I was born and came into the world is to testify to the truth.
Everyone on the side of truth listens to me." And in John 8:31–32, He
tells those who believe in Him, "If you hold to my teaching, you are
really my disciples. Then you will know the truth, and the truth will set
you free." To live like we were created to live, the Bible tells us we need
Jesus. He is the truth, He is life, He came so we would know Him, and

He wants to free us from the conditions of sin and death. When we believe in Him, we have the opportunity to know the greatest heights and depths of love, what is true about life, and how we should live it.

The world was made by God, shaped by Him, and is held together by Him. We can find Jesus in it when we earnestly look and when we observe God's natural order and consider the way He's made us. God has always made Himself available to us. He transcends time and place and has built truth and wisdom into the context of our lives.

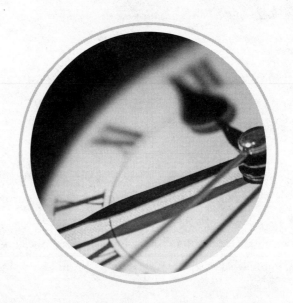

Beyond Time

God's truth stands outside the bounds of time. It was always there, it always will be here, and it is God's. It's constant because God Himself is truth, and He has always existed. From this, we can see that truth operates outside of the confines of the regular physical laws of the universe.

The Bible tells us in 2 Timothy 1:9 that "grace was given us in Christ Jesus before the beginning of time." God's truth is a gift to us, so we can have assurance of who He is, who we are, and what life is all about. He has always loved us and intended for us to know Him.

He also wants us to know His heart. Have you ever read or learned something new, while realizing that it already resonates with you as truth? As God's creation, we were designed with a moral compass to help us tell right from wrong. Even those who don't believe in God have a conscience or moral sense of right and wrong that puts in them a desire to care about or have sympathy for others. And there are certain things, like violence, that even atheists recognize as bad. Most people agree that God's truth, at least to a certain degree, is part of our consciousness because it is hardwired into us.

Years ago when I first began my spiritual journey, I remember reading works by people like C. S. Lewis, Søren Kierkegaard, Siang-Yang Tan, and Gary Moon, all writers, theologians, and thought leaders who lived in different times and contexts. Their words about our design as people and the way we're designed to be in relationship with God not only were consistent and powerful but also resonated with assurances the Holy Spirit was already convicting me of in my heart. I was struck by the fact that they spoke the same truths that were harmonious and unconflicting, recognizable and universal, timeless and relevant. These were truths because they were God's truths, and they always had been.

I've also learned and read from the Bible. It's made up of sixty-six books and written in three languages by more than forty different authors of all different backgrounds over a period of more than fifteen hundred years. You'd think things wouldn't sync up, and yet there's an amazing consistency of truth across all these writings. Collectively, they point the way to Jesus, establishing that He is the way, the truth, and the life. This once again points to the remarkable fact that truth stands outside of time and has everything to do with who God is.

As we contemplate and look to God, the Holy Spirit reveals more and more timeless truth to us. Nothing any contemporary theologians have written is truly original or new; they may phrase things beautifully and poignantly, maybe using a more current presentation style, relatable verbiage, or fresh perspective, but the truths are the same. God's truths have been present since before time began, and what the Bible teaches us about them has always been consistent.

Because "Jesus Christ is the same yesterday and today and forever," as is written in Hebrews 13:8, we can rely on the constancy and changelessness of God's truth. He makes truth known to us through time and has devised our bodies and minds to respond to it. Ephesians 1:4 tells us, "For he chose us in him before the creation of the world to be holy and blameless in his sight." I'm grateful for a God who doesn't leave us to bumble our way through life. He hardwired us for truth and gave us wisdom because He wants to love and save us.

Beyond Place

God's truth is not bound by place or situation, either. It transcends physicality, and we can find it everywhere. In his book *Mere Christianity*, C. S. Lewis writes about universal and eternal truth, saying that if man were to be left alone from interaction or community, away from people in the rest of the world, he would still know right from wrong.[1] He would, according to Lewis, still have not only a conscience to guide him in his own survival but also an innate morality to guide him in his actions, attitudes, and behaviors.

The same is true for us. No matter where we are and what our situation, God has given us a conscience to tell us right from wrong. We have an innate morality that guides us, and whether we listen to it or not, we still hear it. This consciousness of truth is what separates us from animals. And though animals can be amazingly intelligent or demonstrate nurturing, loyalty, collaboration, or other virtues, truth and morality are not built into them in the same way that they are for humans. God's truth and our human conscience link us to God, our Creator; and no matter where we are, truth and morality are applicable to our lives and our purpose.

Sometimes God shows His truth to us through the Bible, through prayer, or through other people. And sometimes, God can guide and encourage us toward His truth using a quiet, gentle, direct voice, speaking into our souls and consciousness, convincing us of something. In 1 Kings 19:11–13, the Bible tells us that Elijah hears God's voice as a gentle whisper. In John 10:27, Jesus says, "My sheep [followers] listen to my voice; I know them, and they follow me." When God talks to us, we hear His message in our head or heart and know it to be true. If we have a relationship with Him and listen for Him, we can recognize His voice and know the truth that comes from His words and character.

In Jeremiah 31:33 and Hebrews 8:10, God says, "I will put my law in their minds and write it on their hearts. I will be their God, and they will be my people." As I mentioned in an earlier chapter, Isaiah 30:21 tells us, "Whether you turn to the right or to the left, your ears will hear a voice behind you, saying, 'This is the way; walk in it.'" God is with us wherever we are. His truth and morality are in us, and He does not leave us alone to figure things out. We start with His law and His way in us, and He directs us. If we're listening for Him, we'll be able to know what's ultimately right.

His Wisdom in Us

We need God's wisdom and guidance in order to live our lives fully, happily, and meaningfully. And from wisdom come hope, goodness, strength, and resilience. I believe God wants good things for our life, so He's made us so that we can know His wisdom.

In the Bible, He gives wisdom to people throughout history, including:

- Moses—"I have filled him with the Spirit of God, with wisdom, with understanding, with knowledge and with all kinds of skills" (Exodus 31:3).

- Joshua—"Now Joshua son of Nun was filled with the spirit of wisdom because Moses had laid his hands on him. So the Israelites listened to him and did what the Lord had commanded Moses" (Deuteronomy 34:9).

- Solomon—"The whole world sought audience with Solomon to hear the wisdom God had put in his heart" (1 Kings 10:24).

These verses show us, among other things, that the Holy Spirit is the one who brings wisdom to people, gives them understanding, and makes it so that other people recognize it. When we love God, we seek to obey Him in the circumstances of our lives. We show an openness and willingness to hear what He has to say and incorporate His ways into our daily living. That's how we become people of wisdom. And as we do, we grow in our relationship with God, improve our own lives, positively impact the lives of others, and cause people to take notice of God's goodness.

Proverbs 3:13 says, "Blessed are those who find wisdom, those who gain understanding." In Ephesians 1:17, Paul prays, "I keep asking that the God of our Lord Jesus Christ, the glorious Father, may give you the Spirit of wisdom and revelation, so that you may know him better." The Bible also tells us that having God's wisdom is a blessing and is something we should try to attain.

As God's created beings, we have His truth built into us and a predisposition for His wisdom. For example, because of the moral compass

God has placed in us, we generally understand that babies need love and nurturing. God, in His wisdom, made us so that we know the basics of caring for a child. We know a child needs to eat, so we provide food. We know a child needs to rest, so we create the conditions for that. We know a child is vulnerable, so we protect them. While we may not find all the logistics easy, we know that even in its most simplistic form, the nurture of a child is necessary in order for it to survive. That knowledge is built in us if we listen to our hearts.

Attachment parenting is a more contemporary parenting philosophy that encourages a secure bond between parents and their children. The concept, though not labeled as such, has been around for thousands of years. In attachment parenting, a parent or primary caregiver keeps a baby close in order to know about and meet her needs. The child receives and feels safe in this love, learning to trust the caregiver. Because the child feels secure and loved, she is confident and resilient enough to explore and learn about her environment and the world. But long before the attachment parenting methodology, parents or primary caregivers built and created bonds with their children through similar means—holding and touching their kids to provide nurture and felt safety, comforting kids with a soothing voice, making eye contact to help kids feel seen and understood. Many parents, including my own mother, practiced these habits because God built into them instincts for nurturing and creating connections. And while this greatly oversimplifies the contemporary definition of attachment parenting, the instincts nonetheless come from the same place, no matter the period in history, no matter the physical locale. Mothers throughout history have nurtured their children; mothers across different continents and with varying cultural backgrounds have and continue to nurture their children. These are instincts not bound by time or place. It's amazing that in His infinite wisdom, God gave people certain instincts for raising children, not only to ensure the survival of the human race but also to create people who could live, thrive, interact, produce, and worship.

D id you know that there's a correlation between faith and health? Harold Koenig, professor of psychiatry and behavioral sciences and associate professor of medicine at Duke University, and director of the Center for Spirituality, Theology, and Health at Duke University Medical Center, has researched and published extensively on the intersection of religion and health. In his book *Handbook of Religion and Health*, he talks about the positive link between religious faith and a person's physical and mental health and well-being, reporting that those who have a strong faith even sometimes live longer. Their immune system works better; they recover more quickly from illness; and they experience less stress, which leads to a decrease in stress-related illnesses.[2] How wise God is to build into our biological mechanisms the ability to be healthier, function better, and live longer through faith. As the quality of our life improves, we can more fully enjoy living out who He created us to be and also have greater opportunity to share God's love and wisdom with others.

God made us, and His signature is on us. He built us to believe in Him, and until we know Him, we'll always feel a need in our hearts for something greater. Whether we realize it or not, our souls long to understand where we came from, where we belong, and how we fit into the big scheme of things. Without those answers—without the truth—we keep on feeling restless, lost, lonely, or unsatisfied. And everything else, good as it may seem at the time, winds up falling short because it's imperfect.

In His goodness, God reaches out to us so we can know His truth. He gives us His Son, shows us the truth through Scripture and historical and eyewitness accounts of Jesus, and enables us to see Him in all sorts of ways, including through signs He's placed throughout His creation. He's put His truth and wisdom into the context of our lives so we might believe in Him and live out the purpose for which we were created.

God also gives us His wisdom generously and graciously. James 1:5 says, "If any of you lacks wisdom, you should ask God, who gives generously to all without finding fault, and it will be given to you." James 3:17 tells us, "But the wisdom that comes from heaven is first of all pure; then peace-loving, considerate, submissive, full of mercy and good fruit, impartial and sincere." God's wisdom is good, full of life, teaching us how to understand Him and love those around us better.

Truth

Truth is truth; it never changes
Remaining the same in all faiths, all languages
It stands outside of time, alone
It brings us peace, carries us back home

Flows as an endless river through every age
Always available, it never lessens or fades
It is there to nourish and to drink
To challenge us to make us think

Truth and wisdom go hand in hand
Cannot separate, conviction it demands
It's in God's heart and His mind
If we seek truth, we will find

—Rhonda Dawes Milner

CHAPTER 10

God's Love and Acceptance

For I am convinced that neither death nor life, neither angels nor demons, neither the present nor the future, nor any powers, neither height nor depth, nor anything else in all creation, will be able to separate us from the love of God that is in Christ Jesus our Lord.

ROMANS 8:38–39

THE FACT THAT WE'RE HERE PROVES GOD LOVES US. FROM a human standpoint, there's no logical reason for our existence on earth. In fact, if we were to calculate or examine things from a scientific point of view, the probability that we would exist is practically nonexistent. Yet, God chose to create the universe, form the earth, fill the earth, and bring human beings and animals to inhabit it with the precision, detail, artistry, genius, innovation, and foresight that only He could. And here we are—proof that we're part of His plan. God made each one of us individually and knows us through and through.

In Romans 11:36 (NLT), the Bible tells us, "For everything comes from Him and exists by his power and is intended for his glory. All glory to him forever! Amen." God created everything, including us, for His glory and to reveal His love. We talked in earlier chapters about how "God made mankind in his own image" (Genesis 1:27) and how each one of us is "fearfully and wonderfully made" (Psalm 139:14). As His image-bearers, we reflect His glory and point to His existence. We are living, breathing examples of His great love and acceptance.

Our Relationship with Him

All of creation points to the reality that God loves us and made us special. It's amazing to think that the God of the universe feels this way about us. The Bible tells us in 1 John 4:19, "We love because he first loved us," and in 1 John 4:10, "This is love: not that we loved God, but that he loved us and sent his Son as an atoning sacrifice for our sins." When we read these verses, as well as others in Scripture, we can see that God's plan has always been to have a relationship with us.

True love between man and woman cannot be created or pretended; you cannot make yourself love someone, nor can you make someone love you. We can choose to love in friendship, but this concept called love is complex. Like our thoughts, we don't truly understand how love works or how it happens. But even though it is something of a mystery, it is the one thing that is the most important in life, as it is everlasting and eternal. True love, on the deep, intimate level, never dies; we may deny or ignore it, but it will remain. This is like God's love for us. We may deny or ignore it, but it is still there, ready for us to receive. It is unfailing and constant, and it connects us to God because God Himself is love.

Many great thinkers and theologians, including St. Augustine, Blaise Pascal, John of the Cross, Søren Kierkegaard, George MacDonald, A. W. Tozer, and C. S. Lewis, have written about our relationship with God. In *The Living Flame of Love*, John of the Cross describes God as the "living flame" who is in the center of our soul; He is there to transform us and is the pursuer, but we must invite Him in.[1] God has made it so that we can choose or not choose to love Him back. Though He doesn't have to, He pursues a relationship with us, and we can opt to either pursue a relationship with Him or not.

As we discussed in an earlier chapter, because of the free will God gave us, we can decide whether we will accept His invitation of a holy love relationship with Him. It would be a contradiction, a dictatorship without autonomy, or even like slavery if our relationship with Him were not one of free choice. Genuinely healthy, loving, and mutually enjoyable relationships with others consist of trust, sacrifice, and give-and-take. These establish intimacy and connection, allowing for us to feel known, bolstering us emotionally, and making us feel secure. How much more so in a relationship with God, who knows us better than anyone, loves and accepts us unconditionally, sacrificed His Son for us, helps us throughout our lives, and promises us we can be loved by Him forever in eternity. Though God does not force us to love Him and gives us a choice, He still made us to know Him, and we work best when we love Him back.

God's relationship model is exemplified through the Trinity of the Father, Son, and Holy Spirit, a harmonious relationship that beautifully demonstrates, among other attributes, God's pure and perfect love. The parts of God in the Trinity are in relationship with one another and are the wellspring from which all love flows. So the concept of a loving, committed relationship, for any of us, originates from the Trinity.

In God's relationship model, He also creates the best love story of all time, a life-changing reality for us through His Son Jesus. John 3:16, one of the most famous Bible verses of all time, captures it beautifully and powerfully: "For God so loved the world that he gave his one and only Son, that whoever believes in him shall not perish but have eternal life." You may have heard this before. The verse essentially tells us this: The good and all-powerful Creator of the universe, the One who sustains it all, loves each and every one of us—people who don't have it together, people who mess up, people who need to be saved from themselves. He offered up His perfect, precious, much-loved, never-failing Son, the *only* Son He has, to pay for our wrongdoing so that we won't have to suffer for our wrongdoing ourselves, which would end in our death and ultimate separation from God. Instead, if we trust in His love and believe Jesus has the power and authority to do this for us, we get to live forever with God in Heaven, a place of love that does not have any sin, suffering, sickness, disaster, or death. This is, as you may have heard it called, the "Gospel." It is, quite literally, what perfect love looks like.

In God's love and acceptance of us, He planned for Jesus to do this for us all along; though once it was realized, it changed the course of history for every human being. This means that in spite of the fact that we sin against Him, He wants to make things right for us and be with us forever. The Gospel is about grace, the reality that we're not getting what we deserve. When we believe in Him, all our offenses from throughout our lifetime will be forgiven, as if we'd lived perfect, sinless lives—even when He knows we didn't (and don't). He rescues us from ourselves and from the effects of the sin of other people in a fallen world. *That's* how much He loves and accepts us.

How We Free Ourselves to Follow Him

God's acceptance of each of us as sinners is a magnanimous gesture of His love. When we feel God's love and acceptance unconditionally and know we are good enough because we are how He made us, we can be set free of the world's judgments and criticisms. And when we feel this and accept the loving relationship we can have with Him, we can be healed, our wounds vanish, and we more fully become who He meant for us to be.

I have a daughter who has struggled with an eating disorder and drug addiction. Having studied addiction and eating disorders in graduate school and working as a doctor and counselor, I've come to understand that the painfulness of each of these afflictions goes deep. Many strategies and treatments can help, but in order to be fully cured from addiction, something more powerful is required. Even if someone struggling with a disorder or addiction could find a way to physically or mentally cope, the painfulness of the heart and soul adds another dimension that also needs healing. Experience has shown me that unless we address all the hurt parts of a person, the wound will still need repair. On this side of Heaven, no healing is complete, apart from what God can do.

So many of us experience deep feelings of shame, guilt, fear, distrust, doubt, insecurity, rejection, inferiority, or despair as well. We can try to repair the situations that cause these feelings, use positive self-talk, or shake them off, but I've found that we truly need God's acceptance in order to genuinely believe we're good enough. Only then do we experience the kind of love and forgiveness we need, feel healing in our souls, and move out of that place of being stuck. Humans are complex, and we have not only many layers of pain but also memories that hold on to the hurts in our lives. With God's forgiveness and healing, we also develop the capacity and desire to extend love and forgiveness to others.

Interestingly, the twelve-step program, a successful program that's widely used to help people recover from addictions, compulsions, and other problems, is built on principles of God's love, acceptance, and forgiveness. Robert Perkinson, a clinical director, psychologist, and counselor who specializes in treating alcoholics, addicts, and pathological gamblers, says in his book *Chemical Dependency Counseling* that for those in Alcoholics Anonymous, a relationship with God is the most important factor to recovery.[2] Once those in the program recognize God's key role in their healing, they're able to move forward, experiencing the freedom and courage to let go of their addictions, surrender their lives to God, forgive those who have hurt them, forgive themselves, and begin making amends to other people they've hurt.

We have much to learn from this. On our own journeys, no matter how big or insurmountable we think our troubles are, nothing should be too big or too much for us to forgive because nothing is too big or too much in us for God to forgive. We are all sinners, and not a single thing we've ever done or will do in our lifetime is a surprise to God; although, because of God's holiness, our sin is what separates us from Him, He loves us and preemptively bridged the gap for us through the sacrifice of His Son Jesus so that we do not need to be separated from Him. If we believe in Jesus, He overcomes the power of sin for us. We can trust that He will make all things right in the end because He is a just God. And we can trust that He will take care of us.

I've found that addiction and many of our problems grow out of a flawed or missing relationship with God. Whether we realize it or not, the things that have a stronghold on us in life often result from unmet needs we have, the desire of our souls to be in a safe, loving relationship with God. When we have a relationship with God and are aligned with His will, the space we try to fill with other things, particularly things we may find ourselves addicted to, is already filled by God; there simply is no room for these things.

God created us to be in relationship with Him. We have been pre-wired in our genetic makeup with a desire for a relationship with Him. On some level, we are conscious of an emptiness within us that nothing else in this world seems to be able to satisfy or fill. It is like trying to fit a square peg into a round hole. In *The Weight of Glory*, C. S. Lewis describes a longing that is inbuilt in all of us, a desire for a relationship with God.[3] James Bryan Smith, director of the Apprentice Institute for Christian Spiritual Formation, theology professor, and author, says that with certain addictions or compulsions, "When we are properly connected to God and his kingdom we find that the void is filled."[4] Blaise Pascal, A. W. Tozer, and other theologians and writers have also recognized this God-space within us. We may try to fill this space with other things—money, power, or any addiction—but these substitutes cannot fill it in the way our souls need; they were not intended to fill it.

In his book *Addiction and Grace*, doctor and psychiatrist Gerald May describes addiction as anything that someone places before God, noting that addiction is essentially idolatry, and everyone struggles with addiction.[5] Since nothing can satisfy or fill the empty hole within us except for the loving relationship we were meant to have with God, we often live in conflict and unrest when we deny the need for God.

God's desire is to give us His life and love abundantly. If we can trust Him with our lives and believe He knows what's best for us, He will satisfy the deepest desires of our hearts, we will find security in His love, and we will realize what our identity was meant to be all along. And in all this, we will experience peace, joy, rest, freedom, and happiness. Amazingly, because of God's love and acceptance, this is what He desires for us.

Godly Relationships with Others

Since we've been offered the greatest love of our lives, how should this inform the way we live? I believe that when we love well, we reflect God. When we accept others in spite of their faults, we reflect God. When we think of others before ourselves, we reflect God. When the reason we do this is because we're grateful He did it for us, we honor Him and bring Him glory.

Though as human beings we'll never be able to love as perfectly as God does, we do feel and experience great love in the relationships He's given us—the love and devotion a parent has for their child, the love and commitment spouses have for one another, and the love and loyalty life-long friends share, for example. Our relationship dynamics are different with each person, but the genuine, selfless love we experience points back to a Creator, the One who showed us love first and who even made that kind of love possible. The love we have for others offers a glimpse of the depth of God's love for us.

After the birth of my first child, I remember wondering how I could possibly ever love any other child as much as I loved her. I felt a powerful, marvelous love that tapped into my very soul and made me see the world differently. As I went on to have three more children, with each one I found, incredibly, that my capacity for love grew, my understanding of what was good and important in the world developed, and I became a better, fuller human being for having the honor of experiencing that kind of love.

With each one of my children, I was also struck by how unique and remarkable they were, with qualities, traits, sensibilities, and gifts particular only to them. It made me wonder how God sees each one of us, who, in His good pleasure, He also made uniquely. No one else in the world is made exactly like us, has the same beginning as us, or feels and responds to those foundations in precisely the way we do. We are shaped and wired a certain way and impacted by the specific circumstances in which we find ourselves. Whatever the unique combination of our personality and ever-changing life situations, God orchestrated it all for a reason. And this is because of His unending capacity for love and His plan to make Himself known to the world through us. It's absolutely amazing to think that when we love people well, His love can flow through us to others.

As we look to God to love and forgive us in our daily lives, we must also look in our hearts to extend love and forgiveness to others. In doing so, we obey God's will. He wants all people to be treated with love and respect. Luke 6:31 says, "Do to others as you would have them do to you." In Matthew 18:21–22, Peter asks Jesus, "Lord, how many times shall I forgive my brother or sister who sins against me? Up to seven times?" Jesus answers, "I tell you, not seven times, but seventy-seven times." Later, in Matthew 22:39, Jesus says that the second greatest commandment is to "Love your neighbor as yourself." These verses point to the fact that we have a responsibility to love others well, showing them the same love we hope to receive ourselves. As we do this, God is blessed.

God wants us to have a relationship with Him and with others. He modeled the way we should love, reaching out to us and sending Jesus to save us from sin. He wants us to follow His example of love and acceptance, and as we do this, to not only show care to other people but also cause them to see God differently. First John 4:16 tells us, "God is love. Whoever lives in love lives in God, and God in them." We honor God when we love Him and allow Him to dwell in our hearts. His desire is that when we have faith in Him, we do our best to help others know His love also.

God's love and His acceptance are evident in our mere existence on planet earth. He could have created the universe in any way He wanted to, altered the conditions on our planet, or made us differently. But none of it is a mistake. He orchestrated it all for His love and for our good. So what should our response be to Him? I believe it is to follow Him, love Him, and help others know they're loved. Psalm 136:1–4 says, "Give thanks to the Lord, for he is good. His love endures forever. Give thanks to the God of gods. His love endures forever. Give thanks to the Lord of lords; His love endures forever. To him alone who does great wonders, His love endures forever." God loves us, and His love for us will never end. For that, I am eternally grateful.

Love's Wellspring

The unselfish, unconditional love
continually flows outward
and overwhelms me.
This love is the purest in the world.
It is given with no expectation.
I know this love of God because of you.
To know that I am because of you is enough.
When I feel unworthy, you are there encouraging.
My unsureness vanishes to your touch.
If you are goodness then I must be the same.
This bond surely cannot break.
Won't I recognize you transformed?
Doesn't the eye know its hand?
Will I know your mother and her mother, too?
It is all connected.
Love is the sum of the parts.
Eternal, enduring, knowing no end,
Love is the wellspring from God's heart.

—Rhonda Dawes Milner

CHAPTER 11

God's Grace and Mercy

For you know the grace of our Lord Jesus Christ, that
though he was rich, yet for your sake he became poor,
so that you through his poverty might become rich.

2 CORINTHIANS 8:9

WHEN GOD MADE THE WORLD, HE KNEW ALREADY THAT we would need His grace and mercy. He accounted for it because that's how much He loves us. And even though He understood that humanity—we—would sin and rebel from Him, He created us anyway and included a plan to rescue us, essentially to save us from ourselves. He knew, in the fallen state of the world, that we would let Him down, turn away from Him, betray Him, not even notice Him. But He wanted us to have a chance to know Him anyway, bringing us to life and going so far as to call us His masterpieces. (The New Living Translation of the Bible describes it like this in Ephesians 2:10: "For we are God's masterpiece. He has created us anew in Christ Jesus, so we can do the good things he planned for us long ago.")

God, who is omniscient and wise, knows everything about us, even our worst or most awful parts, and He loves us with both eyes open, accepting us exactly as we are. This is because of His grace and mercy, which culminated in the person of Jesus Christ, the Son of God who lived, walked, and breathed among us here on earth. We can try to be gracious, forgiving, and loving to one another in life, but we do so imperfectly. Jesus personifies what grace is all about.

The Bible says in John 1:14, "The Word became flesh and made his dwelling among us. We have seen his glory, the glory of the one and only Son, who came from the Father, full of grace and truth." In His mercy, Jesus, often referred to by Christians as the "Word" because He personifies what was spoken and written about Him in the Old Testament, is described as being full of grace and truth. His name is not only synonymous with grace; He embodies it.

God's signature in the world can be seen through His grace and mercy. In fact, I believe the entire universe exists to demonstrate God's goodness, gloriousness, and grace. When we know Him and follow Him, we are changed, and His goodness, gloriousness, and grace can then be seen in us. When we know Him, even as imperfect as we still are, our life and our priorities look different, and we are defined not by what we do (or have done) but by how God sees us. When we decide to trust and follow Jesus, God frees us from the trappings of sin and tells us we are now His own sons and daughters, fully adopted. And all this is because of His grace and mercy.

The Cost of Grace and Mercy

God's grace and mercy were extended to us out of His love for us. We did nothing to earn or merit it. On the contrary, we deserve the opposite. Not one of us, no matter how good we are in life, qualifies for a reward or gift like the one so freely given to us by our Father. As we touched upon in the chapter on God's love and acceptance, not only did God offer an exchange or payment of a ransom for our sins so we could be with Him in eternity, He sacrificed His only Son for us; and His son, because of His love for His Father, gave His life willingly for our salvation and to honor His Father's will. This shows us that the grace we receive from God comes at a great cost. We have it because God, as a Father, gave up His only Son for us. We have it because Jesus, as the Son, gave up His life for us. They knew we needed rescuing, and Jesus was the only one who would be able to fulfill this price for all humankind. So He obeyed His Father, demonstrated the ultimate love and sacrifice for us, and accomplished the purpose for which He'd been sent to earth. It was an extravagant price to pay for both Father and Son.

In Matthew 17:5, the Father announces, "This is my Son, whom I love; with him I am well pleased." The Maker of the universe and all of creation tells us, with this special declaration, that He loves His Son and is happy about Him. In John 3:16, He also refers to Jesus as "his one and only Son." This means there are no others; Jesus is special, and it costs the Father something to give up His only child, knowing His child would need to endure suffering and death for every human being in history. Though He was grieved by the pain and suffering Jesus would have to go through for us, God knew this was the only way to rescue us from sin. God saw to the fact that things would work for our good. He created us in love and has prepared a way that we could be justified by grace through faith in Him. Romans 8:31 ends with this powerful truth: "If God is for us, who can be against us?" If the God who created everything in the universe has extended His love, grace, mercy, peace, and protection to us, nothing can defeat us when we believe in Jesus and have an identity in Him.

At the same time, the grace and mercy we freely receive from Jesus also came at an enormous cost to Him. Our gain was His complete and utter loss, and this is a hard reality with deep implications for us. Jesus endured the deepest suffering anyone in all of history has ever endured. Among other things, He was painfully betrayed by people who were close to Him, abandoned and rejected by those who said they loved Him, unjustly accused by Jewish leaders, tortured and abused by Roman soldiers, pierced with a spear, crucified, and made to experience the ultimate in agony: total and complete separation from God. Crucifixion was a slow, agonizing form of death, devised because other forms were thought to be too quick. Since the penalty for our sins is death, Jesus needed to physically die for us. But with death also comes a spiritual separation from God; in dying for us, Jesus not only went through the agony of being separated from God, He went through the actual agony of hell.

Matthew 26:39 tells us that right before Jesus is taken into custody and made to endure all this, He asks His Father in Gethsemane, "My Father, if it is possible, may this cup be taken from me. Yet not as I will, but as you will." In this same moment, Luke 22:44 tells us, "And being in anguish, he prayed more earnestly, and his sweat was like drops of blood falling to the ground." Jesus knows what He's about to take on, and it's so spiritually and emotionally distressing for Him that Luke, the physician who is the writer of the book of Luke, describes Jesus as experiencing something called hematidrosis, a rare condition in which tiny capillaries in the sweat glands rupture from stress, causing a person to physically sweat blood. Jesus, as we know, willingly went on to obey His mission in life: to go to the Cross for all of humanity and save us. He came in bodily form to suffer and die in our place, to take the punishment for our sins, and to literally go to hell for us.

Jesus paid an extravagant price for us, but He believes we're worth it. Surrounding all this, John 15:13 says, "Greater love has no one than this: to lay down one's life for one's friends." Matthew 20:28 tells us, "The Son of Man did not come to be served, but to serve, and to give his life as a ransom for many." So in the grace and mercy that God extends *to* us in Christ, Christ graciously took on our sins and paid the penalty for the sin *in* us *for* us. The Bible tells us He died, descended to hell, rose on the third day, was resurrected from the dead, and after forty days, ascended into Heaven to sit at the right hand of our Father. He died for everyone who has ever walked on earth, so we could all have a chance to go to Heaven and be with God. The penalty for our sin is death, but if we believe Jesus did these things for us and had the power to come alive again, actually defeating death, we can be saved from death ourselves. His grace and mercy will be ours, and we can choose to accept Him and be in relationship with Him.

Walking in Grace and Mercy

We need Jesus every day in order to know how to live, move, act, think, and be. This doesn't mean we're helpless, mindless people simply because we've chosen to recognize God as the Creator of the universe and lover of our souls. He's made us who He's made us; we have our own wills, we have our sensibilities, we have our personalities. He's wired us each uniquely for a reason, and that makes Him happy. When we claim our identity in Him, we live the way we were always meant to live and are most fully who He always created us to be. He *wants* us to be who we are and live out our legacy.

This is challenging, though, and you've undoubtedly seen many people—non-Christians and Christians alike—who do their own thing, exclusive of the way God may be wanting them to live. We live in a fallen world, not yet in Heaven, and are faced every moment with not only our own sins but also the sins of other people and the state of the world. Thank goodness for God's grace and mercy. Thank goodness for the price Jesus already paid for us. As we go about our daily lives, it's nearly impossible not to be influenced or corrupted by sin. But God knows this, and that's why He came in advance for us. He's made it so that even as we struggle in an imperfect world, we can live lives of purpose, peace, and meaning and have hope for the perfect Heaven to come.

I believe this takes an everyday surrendering of our spirit and will to God, a constant request to Jesus for help to keep sin from our lives. We can ask God's Holy Spirit to spiritually fill our souls and sensibilities so that we can journey through each moment in His grace and mercy. And even as sin is there, we can trust and believe He already took care of it for us and be renewed. There's something supernatural with the way this works, and it probably sounds far-fetched to those who don't believe in Jesus, but it's a beautiful, powerful, humbling reality that we feel deeply when we walk in faith. It takes a willingness to step out and trust that Jesus is who He says He is and accept that the signs He's left for us in creation and in our lives are true; when this happens, He meets us the rest of the way, filling us with hope, conviction, gratitude, and love. When we receive Him, we reflect His grace and mercy.

Turning to God

God, who is pure goodness and love, cannot allow sin in His presence, so the only way we could ever be allowed into eternity or Heaven with God is to be without sin. Since any sin, no matter how seemingly small, is still sin, it would be impossible for us to get to Heaven on our own merit. Again, we live in a fallen world, sin is part of our built-in nature, and we simply will never be able to be perfect all the time. But, the good news is that no sin is too big for God to forgive; in fact, He already did in Jesus. All we need is a heart that is repentant of sin and that yields to the God who took care of it for us. Isaiah 55:7 says, "Let them turn to the Lord, and he will have mercy on them, and to our God, for he will freely pardon." Hebrews 4:16 says, "Let us then approach God's throne of grace with confidence, so that we may receive mercy and find grace to help us in our time of need." And in 2 Timothy 1:9, we are reminded, "He has saved us and called us to a holy life—not because of anything we have done but because of his own purpose and grace. This grace was given us in Christ Jesus before the beginning of time." When we turn to God, approach Him, and seek a good, holy life, He freely gives us grace and mercy.

God Is with Us

God is with us every step of the way. When Jesus was sent to earth to save us, He came as a helpless baby who was born into squalid, humble circumstances. He grew into a man who suffered pain and hurt, just as we might in our own flesh and hearts. Because of having lived on earth Himself, He can tangibly identify with the human experience. He truly knows and understands our pain and suffering in every sense.

Although we live in a sinful, fallen world and can't avoid pain and suffering, Jesus promises to walk closely with us in every moment. There is grace and mercy in the fact that we are never alone, even in our darkest or most sorrowful times. Deuteronomy 31:6 tells us we can "be strong and courageous. Do not be afraid or terrified because of them, for the Lord your God goes with you; he will never leave you nor forsake you." Joshua 1:5 assures us, "No one will be able to stand against you all the days of your life. As I was with Moses, so I will be with you; I will never leave you nor forsake you." And again, God tells us in Hebrews 13:5, "Never will I leave you; never will I forsake you."

God is always here to give us comfort and strength because He knows what lies ahead for us in our lives. He will never abandon or forget us. We can take heart in that.

At the same time, God has given us His Holy Spirit to help us. When we believe in God, we're filled with His Spirit, and the love and goodness of God can be seen in us. The Holy Spirit moves among us, stirring our souls, comforting us, teaching us, bolstering us, guiding us, interceding for us, helping us to become who we were created to be. It's amazing that when the Holy Spirit comes to us as believers, we're connected to God, the source of love, the Maker of the universe. And not only does God's Spirit help us in our own lives, but with His Spirit in us, we become God's conduit, making it so that His light is able to also shine through us for the world to see. Galatians 5:22–25 says, "But the fruit of the Spirit is love, joy, peace, forbearance, kindness, goodness, faithfulness, gentleness and self-control. Against such things there is no law. Those who belong to Christ Jesus have crucified the flesh with its passions and desires. Since we live by the Spirit, let us keep in step with the Spirit." When we have an identity in Jesus and seek to keep in step with Him, "the fruit of the Spirit" can be seen in us; guided by His Spirit, we can't help but to reflect His love, joy, peace, patience, kindness, goodness, faithfulness, gentleness, and self-control. These natural effects of His Spirit in us are displays of His signature in our lives.

This is God's goodness and grace to us. And as His believers, we can't help but to become His agents of grace in the world around us when we earnestly seek Him and have an authentic faith.

Trusting God

We were made to trust in God. As the everlasting God who made all of time, He knows that in the biggest scheme of things, our life on earth happens in just the blink of an eye compared to the reality of time that stretches out for all of eternity. He is Himself eternity and yet is able to also be simultaneously here in the present moment. He loves us and wants us to understand that He has always known how He made us and had our best interests at heart. And He gave us souls that transcend beyond our physical bodies or time here on earth; we're made to love, trust, and worship Him, not only now but also for all of eternity.

I'm always awed to think of the way He designed our existence just so we can see Him—in the world around us, in science and nature, in our circumstances, and in our own human experience. He gave us the true story of who He is in the Bible and sent His Holy Spirit to dwell with us. He Himself, through His Son Jesus, physically descended from Heaven to meet us, providing a bridge to Him that we otherwise wouldn't be able to cross on our own. This is an incredible gift to us that He didn't have to give. But as a gracious God, He did it so we wouldn't have to be lost, alone, or condemned.

Becoming Like Christ

The Bible says in 1 John 3:1, "See what great love the Father has lavished on us, that we should be called children of God! And that is what we are!" When we become a Christian, we are described as children of God because God loves us and considers us as His own sons and daughters. Think of that. The sovereign, mighty, all-powerful, all-knowing, timeless Creator of the universe cares about us enough to bring us into His family and think of us as His own children. We become His heirs, with all the birthrights and unending love a good parent would have for their child. We are protected, cherished, and known, and there's nothing our parent wouldn't do for us.

In light of that, writer and theologian George MacDonald talks in his book *Your Life in Christ* about how we might also think of Jesus as an older brother and role model.[1] As we do this, we become more obedient to God's will and way, honoring Him with the way we live our lives and pointing others to God with the example of Christ. We become conformed to the loving image of Jesus and act as His representatives in the world, so others may come to know how much they are loved as well.

To become more like Christ means we are, with the help of God's Holy Spirit, growing in our faith and learning how to live out the legacy for which we were created. Writer, philosopher, and contemporary theologian, Dallas Willard, uses the term "Christlikeness" to talk about a believer's spiritual transformation. In *The Spirit of the Disciplines*, he says we are not just to do as Jesus does but to live as Jesus lived.[2] This is made possible as the Holy Spirit draws us nearer and nearer to God in the love and intimacy that develops when we get to know God more and discover what it means to live our lives for Him.

In *The Practice of the Presence of God*, Brother Lawrence, widely known as a deeply spiritual man in the Church, writes that we can walk in God's presence in everything we do, even in the most simple and mundane of tasks, if we do it for the love of God.[3] I believe we are called, as Brother Lawrence might say, to live life from the inside out, where our spiritual life is manifest in everything we do in the physical world. Colossians 1:27 reads, "To them God has chosen to make known among the Gentiles the glorious riches of this mystery, which is Christ in you, the hope of glory." To be Christlike, reflecting His true grace and mercy, we live *in* and *through* Christ, and He lives *in* and *through* us. As this happens, we are able to claim our inheritance of the Kingdom of God as a child of God.

Jesus says in Matthew 22:37–38, "Love the Lord your God with all your heart and with all your soul and with all your mind. This is the first and greatest commandment." He asks us to love Him well and with everything we've got. Because of the grace and mercy He's shown us, we are not only grateful to be forgiven for our sins but also compelled to share our joy about this to others. As we do this, even with the most humble of actions, we shine His light and His grace and mercy into the world. He freely gives grace and mercy to us in all generosity, and we are so overwhelmed by this that we can't help but to extend it to others out of the surplus we've received. My prayer of grace for you, from 2 Thessalonians 2:16–17, is this: "May our Lord Jesus Christ himself and God our Father, who loved us and by his grace gave us eternal encouragement and good hope, encourage your hearts and strengthen you in every good deed and word."

The Space

What is in the space?
That separates God from the human race
Is it life in Heaven juxtaposed to life on earth?
Never to be closed until time's end
When new earth begins renews us again

What is the space?
Is it the permanent separation from God of sin
What blocks entry to Heaven not letting us in
That we turn to each and every day
When we fall and lose our way

What is in the space?
Our humanness spilling over through
centuries and years
Imperfections, failings, emotions, fears
Only angels tread lithely traverse this gap
For the empty callous there is no guide or map

What is in the space?
Our lack of faith and disbelief
Our hardened hearts filled with grief

No trust in the invisible eternal unseen
Minds laughing mocking at this pretend dream

What closes the space?
That joins God with the human race, our hearts aim
Our yearning, longing for our permanent domain
Man's search for meaning and connection
Our desire for unending love, attachment,
and affection

What closes the space?
God who breathed life into all nature and creation
Who created man as a wonder filled with knowledge
and so many sensations
In the beginning was just Him, the Three in One
This love surely is manifest through the Son

What closes the space?
The Christ child who became man
Who brought healing and faith to all lands
Who died for us on a cross
He sacrificed for us so we would not be lost

What closes the space?
The Holy Spirit as He who was left
He is the one who now safely keeps us kept
Man seeking God Him waiting to be found
Jesus bridges this space He wears the glory and the crown

—*Rhonda Dawes Milner*

CHAPTER 12

God's Blessings and Affirmations

*And my God will meet all your needs accord-
ing to the riches of his glory in Christ Jesus.*

PHILIPPIANS 4:19

BLESSINGS ARE GOD'S FAVOR AND PROTECTION IN OUR
lives. They are an expression of His goodness and care, and He uses them
to help and encourage us. Through them, He guides us, emboldens us,
buoys us, carries us, and lifts us up in spirit. God has always shown us
special favor and affirmed us through His blessings. I believe He delights
in bestowing good on us because it's a way of showing He loves us and is
drawing us close to Him. It's also how He carries out His purpose in the
world through us.

The fact that we're blessed by God also says something about His
strength, wisdom, and power. He has blessings to give us because He's
greater than we are and has the ability to do this. His blessings highlight
His supremacy at the same time that they communicate something about
our humanness and need. Ephesians 1:3 says, "Praise be to the God and

Father of our Lord Jesus Christ, who has blessed us in the heavenly realms with every spiritual blessing in Christ." God blesses all of us, whether we have a personal relationship with Him or not. But when we choose to follow Him, His blessings play out profoundly in our lives, sometimes in ways we may not even recognize.

When we see blessings in our lives, do we see Him? Or do we receive the effects of God's favor and protection and attribute them to something else? James 1:17 tells us, "Every good and perfect gift is from above, coming down from the Father of the heavenly lights." I believe we live and breathe under God's blessings. Like signs of Him in all of creation, they point to evidence of a good, kind, omniscient God who has the power to act, the desire to bring joy to our lives, and the longing for us to know Him.

Noticing God's Blessings

In thinking through the different experiences in my life, taking a closer look at Scripture, and reflecting on what it all means and how it connects, I've come to believe that a spiritual reality exists within us. As compared to our physical and bodily realm, which we know is temporary here on earth, there is an eternal realm, invisible to our naked eye yet nonetheless felt deeply in our souls. Something is alive and beautiful, unique and significant in us, something more than the simple biology of cells (though that is also amazing). God connects with us and blesses us through both of these realms because, as the timeless, omnipresent Creator of the universe, He's everywhere and always has been.

His signature is on all of creation and on us, and He chooses to make Himself known through His blessings. Though, as a good and all-knowing God, He personally blesses and affirms us in ways that we may not even understand, He also blesses us all the time in our physical and spiritual realities in ways we can actually observe. All we need is to have our God antenna up so that we can receive His wonderful gifts of love. To find Him, we need eyes not only to look but to see, and ears not only to hear but to listen.

God speaks to us in our physical realm in order to reach our spiritual realm, and as I describe in earlier chapters, many times this happens through His creation. I believe nature can be sacramental, as an outward, visible sign of an invisible, spiritual grace of God, something my spiritual director once so beautifully described to me. If you're open and receptive to it, you may experience the incarnational—the eternal spiritual realm revealed in the temporal physical realm. What God does around us and in our lives stirs up hope in our souls, offers us encouragement, helps us find resiliency, and gives us patience and strength. These are intangible spiritual blessings in us that are brought on by tangible, physical blessings around us. The Holy Spirit helps us to process and understand these in ways that resonate with us, that are meaningful, and that, perhaps, could even be life changing. And the response this evokes in us is one of wonder and worship.

I'm grateful for the way God affirms me through the blessings He works into my life, and I'm humbled that He would even speak to my soul in this way. For some reason, the God of the universe—who doesn't *need* to affirm us—*wants* to affirm us. He wants us to understand that He's there, that He knows who we are (because He made us), and that He loves us. To be adored like that by someone who doesn't have to do it is amazing.

God bolsters us through His blessings and, when we believe in Him, offers us a way out of sin. As we experience these gifts from Him, I pray we're encouraged to live our lives better and to live our lives for Him, our Father and our Maker. Hebrews 12:1 says, "Therefore, since we are surrounded by such a great cloud of witnesses, let us throw off everything that hinders and the sin that so easily entangles. And let us run with perseverance the race marked out for us." Let us, knowing God is with us, encourage and spur one another on toward God and the life we have always been meant to live. We have and can be part of the great cloud of witnesses, cheering us all on to victory.

God's Constant Blessing

The fact that we can't always see what God is doing in our life doesn't mean He isn't blessing us. A fact of human nature and part of living in a fallen world is that we often focus more of our attention on the effects of God's blessings than we do on Him as the Blesser. Sometimes we are so fixated on our circumstances that we don't think of God. And other times, when things go wrong, we may tend to believe we're *not* being blessed by God much at all. Our inclination may be to assume God is withholding His favor or punishing us in some way. This has happened in my life, but in actuality, I understand now how God has used these experiences to change me and grow me into something better. He has been able to transform my sorrow into song.

The Bible tells us that God always blesses His believers. His love is constant, and when we choose to follow Him, we can trust that He's actively working on our behalf. Psalm 84:11 tells us, "For the Lord God is a sun and shield; the Lord bestows favor and honor; no good thing does he withhold from those whose walk is blameless." Since the beginning of time, God has engineered our circumstances to show us His love and favor and to draw us close to Him. He has signed His name on all of creation for us to see and notice. And knowing that we would not be able to walk blamelessly on our own strength or by our own virtue, He sent us His Son Jesus to bridge the gap for us. In the sacrifice of Christ, God counts us as blameless. He is a God of blessing.

God also blesses those who do not yet know Him. We know that in John 3:16, the Bible tells us, "For God so loved the world that he gave his one and only Son, that whoever believes in him shall not perish but have eternal life." Jesus died for the world, for people everywhere. He died to offer freedom from sin and salvation for anyone who wants it, and He did not discriminate in this. He also shapes and works circumstances to show people that He's there. His signature in creation is evident for all to see, regardless of whether we know Him or not. Again, He is a God of blessing.

Blessings in Disguise

People tend to think of financial success or worldly comfort as indications that God is blessing them in life. The purchase of a big house, an acceptance into a university, a fancy vacation, a promotion at work, recognition for a major accomplishment, or the acquiring of a car are circumstances that might cause people to think about how "blessed" they are. And all of these *can*, in fact, be wonderful blessings. But does this mean when things go wrong or our circumstances are less than ideal that God isn't working in our lives or blessing us? When we are going through difficult times, yet someone else seems to have everything going for them, are they being blessed while we are not?

I believe that it isn't only those with big homes, expensive cars, great marriages, many friends, perfect health, or high-paying jobs who are blessed. And it isn't only those who seem to have no problems in life that God is affirming. Sometimes those whose lives look to be a total mess are being blessed in profound and beautiful ways. I've learned from my own life that when things aren't perfect or we're going through pain is when we can most deeply experience God's blessings. In the act of asking God for help and our need to cry out to Him, *that's* when we're often being blessed and affirmed in a special way. In these times, when we pull close to God, recognizing Him as the one who can give us strength, heal us, or deliver us from our troubles, we feel loved, we grow in our faith, and we find a peace that surpasses understanding and transcends our situation. I've found that when I trust God fully, blessings, beauty, goodness, and peace grow out of my difficult situations, though this may be completely counterintuitive to how things seem to work in the world.

Isaiah 61:3 describes a situation in which God provides for those who need help, saying He will "bestow on them a crown of beauty instead of ashes, the oil of joy instead of mourning, and a garment of praise instead of a spirit of despair. They will be called oaks of righteousness, a planting of the Lord for the display of his splendor." God alone has the ability to reach into the deepest parts of our soul to bring beauty from ashes, transform sadness into joy, and give us a heart of praise rather than one trapped in despair. James 1:12 says, "Blessed is the one who perseveres under trial because, having stood the test, that person will receive the crown of life that the Lord has promised to those who love him." I find this to be particularly powerful. People don't generally wish for difficult trials in life (or ashes, mourning, or despair), but God helps us and says that when we stand strong and persevere, we're not only blessed but will receive the crown of life He's promised us.

What if our pain, sorrow, and suffering are God's invitation to draw us closer to Him and are actually His blessings? I've experienced much pain and suffering in life, including childhood traumas and abuse, great personal hardship, seemingly insurmountable challenges, and tremendous loss.

Looking back on my life, the most difficult and challenging circumstances for me weren't the personal traumas but the pain and suffering my children have experienced. God can often get our attention through our children, who hold our heartstrings. My younger daughter was three months premature, and many times we almost lost her. This was a time in my life when my heart felt fragile and vulnerable. But, God used this time to make me open up to Him, and I became "born again" on Easter Sunday 1990, realizing Jesus Christ was and is my Savior.

Then, my older daughter developed an eating disorder, which became life threatening, requiring her to be hospitalized and sent away for treatment at the age of thirteen. Sadly, her eating disorder subsequently led to a drug addiction to heroin, something that has almost taken her life multiple times. But, God's blessing in this was that, knowing CPR, I was able to resuscitate her after discovering her lifeless and not breathing. I felt as if, to be able to save my daughter's life, I had become a physician for precisely that point in time. Today, she is in recovery and also has a beautiful faith that has helped her survive.

My older son had trials and tribulations while going through college, which I shared earlier in the book. The challenges he faced grew him into a wonderful young man of character and faith. I was blessed to see him happy and thriving in life up until the time of his death from practicing breath-holding in our family pool. Nothing could ever have prepared me for finding him dead. But this time, my child could not be brought back from the clutches of death. From my sorrow, pain, and desire to spare others the loss of a loved one from underwater breath-holding arose our organization to prevent shallow water blackout.

God has blessed me through these hardships so that I could grow closer to Him, know that He alone is my strength and salvation, and trust that He can bring good from the worst of circumstances. I never expected that I would find myself in the position of choosing to bring good from an awful tragedy. But with God, all things are possible.

Since my son's death, I have experienced the blessing of holding both anguish and joy at the same time and having joy in the midst of sorrow. I have been given affirmations of God's love and affirmations of eternal life. These experiences range from finding pennies from Heaven to red cardinals, dragonflies, yellow butterflies, tree frogs, doves, feathers, or rainbows—objects of personal significance to me, unexplainable experiences and coincidences that speak of a loving, caring, supernatural God. I believe God speaks into our physical realm through His creation, leaving His signature on us and around us. If we are open, we may experience the incarnational, the eternal, spiritual realm being revealed in our temporal realm. And if we have our God antenna up, we can receive these wonderful gifts of love and affirmation. But we must have eyes to not only look but to see, and ears not only to hear but to listen. Some people call these signs and experiences *God winks*. I call them *God kisses*.

While I wish I had not gone through all of this, I also recognize that today I am more of the person I was always meant to be because of these trials. Everything that happened has been an affirmation of God's love and presence and a confirmation that I am following His chosen path for me. I've grown to be a stronger person. And I don't know that I would have the same spiritual perspective or sense of peace had I not experienced the kind of difficulty I endured in the past. God is faithful in the midst of pain.

The message of my story is not that pain or suffering disappear when we know God, but rather that He transforms it. He transforms *us* in difficult circumstances, and that's a way of blessing us. As Romans 8:28 reminds us, "And we know that in all things God works for the good of those who love him, who have been called according to his purpose." He is faithful. He brings good from our difficult situations, and He uses these to draw us closer to Him. As we rely on and trust Him, even in the midst of our hardest times, He blesses us, promising to provide for us, assuring us He will never forsake us. Our hurts, anxieties, and distress can be blessings in disguise, gifts from God. Blessings are the silver linings of adversity.

Spiritual blessings outweigh and are far better than worldly blessings. We shouldn't look only to the world or other people in order to be comforted, to be affirmed, or to have our deepest needs met. All these things can be lovely, but we'll ultimately come up short if we don't look to God to fulfill our needs. He's the only one who has the power and ability to reach into the deepest parts of our soul. We are blessed by God so that we can love and worship Him more, live at our best and in His will, and become more Christlike.

Blessed to Bless

We can do nothing to deserve God's blessings, and yet He continues to pour them out on us. Because of Him, we have an endless supply of joy, help, peace, and affirmation. Hopefully, His blessings bring us to a place of gratefulness, causing us to draw nearer to God and compelling us to share His goodness with others. I believe one reason God blesses us is so that we can bless others. When we are ourselves a blessing to others, His love flows through us and we point the way to God. In this way, we honor Him and bless Him back.

In Genesis 12:2, God says, "I will make you into a great nation, and I will bless you; I will make your name great, and you will be a blessing." We can (and should) use our blessings—including our resources, time, gifts, and strengths—to be a blessing to those around us and the world. The passage 2 Corinthians 1:3–4 reads, "Praise be to the God and Father of our Lord Jesus Christ, the Father of compassion and the God of all comfort, who comforts us in all our troubles, so that we can comfort those in trouble with the comfort we ourselves receive from God." God tells us He will help us and then asks us to take the comfort we've received from Him to help others. To be honest, God is powerful and capable enough; He doesn't need our help. And yet He gives us the chance to share who He is to others. It's a privilege that He wants us to participate in—showing people how much He loves them and how they can know Jesus.

Philippians 2:3–4 tells us, "Do nothing out of selfish ambition or vain conceit. Rather, in humility value others above yourselves, not looking to your own interests but each of you to the interests of others." I encourage you to not hoard your blessings or forget about God, the giver of every good thing. Consider those who need Him and how you might freely give to others—whether through encouragement, a meal, your friendship, comfort, a kind word, financial support, or any other means—simply because He has lavished so much on you.

In 2 Corinthians 9:8, we read, "And God is able to bless you abundantly, so that in all things at all times, having all that you need, you will abound in every good work." May we, having all that we need, abound in every good work for the glory of God and the benefit of others. And as we bless others, may we experience God's pleasure, knowing we're living as He hopes we would. God affirms us when we carry out His will.

God holds nothing back from loving you. Take heart in that fact and remember that no matter your circumstance, He is always with you, and you lack nothing.

A Love Story

I live and move in Your love
It is Your promised union and covenant
In the Holy Spirit's sign of the white dove
So I am Yours; You are my beloved

You exist in every breath I make
Each moment I give praise while awake
Every night I pray my soul You will take
In my heart I know you will not forsake

I serve You however You wish and say
I follow You to guide and lead my way
You know and number each one of my days
Wherever you lead me I will rest and lay

My soul is Yours and Yours alone
You will forever be my destiny, my true home
I will never be lost, left to aimlessly roam
I will not be afraid, cry, or groan

As a fleeting blade of grass to mere dust
Brief meaning and purpose, find I must

My spirit for You, my love, it only lusts
In you I place all my faith and trust

It is for You my heart longs and yearns
It is from your Words I desire to grow and learn
With this faith, I have no fear, no concerns
It is toward You I move and turn

So I am freed by Your loving grace in
Your merciful sacrifice
Your bloodshed was sufficient; it did suffice
You know my true heart no need to disguise
For our love story, You paid the ultimate price

—*Rhonda Dawes Milner*

CHAPTER 13

God's Joy and Hope

But let all who take refuge in you be glad; let them
ever sing for joy. Spread your protection over them,
that those who love your name may rejoice in you.

PSALM 5:11

JOY IS A HUGE PART OF THE CHRISTIAN LIFE. THIS DOESN'T
mean our circumstances are easy or we don't have troubles. But God gives
us joy—in a supernatural way—that transforms any situation into one
in which we can see Him, know His goodness, and trust in the fact that
things will be okay. Our joy comes from realizing that the glorious, holy,
almighty God of the universe cherishes us; Jesus took our sin away; and
God gave us His Holy Spirit to advocate for us. Our joy comes from
knowing that God not only carries us through but also is bigger than any
and every situation. And our joy comes from understanding that in Him
is victory and the hope of Heaven.

Hope is also a huge part of the Christian life. It's the assurance that
what we expect to have happen will actually happen one day; specifically,
it's the promise of Heaven, deliverance from the fallen state of the world,
the reality that we will be in the perfect and glorious place where God

dwells. Our hope comes from knowing God is with us and for us during our time on earth and that He invites us to be with Him for all eternity when our time here is done. And our hope is built on confidence in a loving and present God, not on wishful thinking about things that might or might not come to pass.

I believe God extends hope to all those who need it; this gives us much to be joyful about in life. Psalm 32:11 says, "Rejoice in the Lord and be glad, you righteous; sing, all you who are upright in heart!" This verse tells us that as believers in Christ, we can be joyful and glad. The emotions we experience when we have God's hope come from a spiritual place, and they elicit a joyful, expressive response. Deuteronomy 26:11 (NLT) tells us, "Go and celebrate because of all the good things the Lord your God has given to you and your household." When we consider all that God has given us, we feel a deep gratefulness and want to enjoy, even celebrate, that feeling. God *tells* us to celebrate His goodness; He takes pleasure in taking care of us and giving us what we need in life. With such a giving, loving God bolstering us in our lives, we are tremendously blessed.

The God of the universe and Maker of all things did not create us to have us fend for ourselves. He has made Himself known to us and is so faithful in the way He interacts with us. When we choose to follow Him, we feel His presence in our hearts, lives, and situations. His signature is on us and evidenced in the hope and joy He so freely gives to us.

Experiencing Joy in Difficult Times

In a fallen world, filled with sin and sadness, we have a light of hope. The story does not end with sin; there's more to life. And God, who wants a relationship with us, gives us the hope of Heaven and promise of joy for all eternity when we believe in Jesus. We know, as we trust

Him, follow Him, and receive His grace, that the ending of our story will turn out beautifully and precisely as He intended. Luke 10:20 tells us to "rejoice that your names are written in heaven." God knows us, and when we choose to know Jesus, He has a place saved for us in eternity with Him. We can take heart and have hope in the best possible outcome for our lives.

When we go through pain and suffering, it's hard to feel a sense of joy and hope. I know this well on a personal level. But I also know the joy and hope God extends are very much there, and I believe any anguish, heartbreak, and pain in our lives can be transformed into joy by God. In my own life, as I've shared, I've experienced tremendous grief. But even in the midst of some of my darkest times when I didn't know how I would go on, God allowed me to find joy and hope.

My grief and pain are still with me; they're a part of who I am. But they are not greater than the deep wells of joy, goodness, peace, and hope God has given me. Isaiah 58:11 says, "The Lord will guide you always; he will satisfy your needs in a sun-scorched land and will strengthen your frame. You will be like a well-watered garden, like a spring whose waters never fail." Emotionally, I still live in a sun-scorched land in this fallen world, and it's hard; but God continues every day—every moment—to give me great strength, and I am, in fact, like a well-watered garden and a spring whose waters never fail. I never forget that He is the one who not only sustains me through my pain but also gives me all that I need to live a full, meaningful life right now. And I can't believe I get to have joy and hope simply because He cares about me that much.

Since my son's death, again and again I've received joy in the midst of sorrow. When we trust God's love for us, this is our reality. Psalm 30:11–12 says, "You turned my wailing into dancing; you removed my sackcloth and clothed me with joy, that my heart may sing your praises and not be silent. Lord my God, I will praise you forever." Psalm 94:19

says, "When anxiety was great within me, your consolation brought me joy." During our most painful losses and hardest times, God's love and provision are there. He not only soothes our feelings or heals our hearts, but He brings us true joy.

Looking Forward with Hope

In the Bible, Paul writes in 2 Corinthians 4:17, "For our light and momentary troubles are achieving for us an eternal glory that far outweighs them all." His statement isn't making light of the suffering or heartache we endure in life; it acknowledges that in the big scheme of things, amazingly, even these things will seem small when compared to what awaits us as His believers. We can trust in the eternity to come—and because of that, we have hope. And that hope brings us peace, gives us resilience, soothes our souls, quiets our hearts, and brings us comfort. With hope, we are able to see past our difficult moments and look forward with joy to what has been promised.

Hebrews 6:19 states, "We have this hope as an anchor for the soul, firm and secure." I have this image that I am a little sailboat, sailing on life's waters. Sometimes the waters are calm, but sometimes stormy seas make life difficult to navigate and stay afloat. I may get tossed and turned, almost even capsizing at times; but with my strong centerboard, I am able to remain upright, not sinking. This strong centerboard for me is my Savior, Jesus Christ. In the same light, Christ is our anchor and hope that keeps us from drifting out to sea or off course. Our hope and promise is in Him. When we keep this focus at the center of our lives, we have assurance that God will keep us upright and anchored through the storms of life.

As much as we would like to, we cannot control our circumstances and what happens to us in life, but we do get to choose where we turn and in whom we place our trust and hope. When we turn to God in earnest, even in the midst of our messes and imperfections, and stay focused on Him, He transforms our hearts and shifts our perspectives. We hold the paradoxes; as the ordinary becomes extraordinary, our pain becomes our solace, our anguish becomes our joy, our sorrow becomes our song. And our faith becomes our hope.

I shared Isaiah 61:3 with you earlier because this verse and promise bring me so much comfort. In it, I'm reminded that God can shine through my troubles. Even as my life is sometimes overtaken with the ashes, mourning, and despair it describes, I can choose to see Him, guiding me through my circumstances, big enough to handle all my problems, caring enough to heal my pain, good enough to bring me hope and joy. I pray for Him to be present with all of us in our times of pain, suffering, and need.

Zephaniah 3:17 tells us, "The Lord your God is with you, the Mighty Warrior who saves. He will take great delight in you; in his love he will no longer rebuke you, but will rejoice over you with singing." In 1 John

4:16, the Bible tells us, "And so we know and rely on the love God has for us. God is love. Whoever lives in love lives in God, and God in them."

God's focus is on eternity—to have us with Him in His Kingdom forever—not the temporary nature of our world. We are His objects of love. As God is love, love that is eternal and everlasting, His heart is the wellspring of love. God loves us and wants what is best for us, even if it is not what we desire. But God sees the big picture that we cannot see. He is pure love, so He can only love us. When a parent truly and deeply loves a child, they want what is best for the child and do everything they can to make sure that best happens. How much more so with God, our Father, our Maker, the lover of our souls. As John 3:16 tells us, God so loved the world that He gave His only Son so that we may know everlasting life with Him.

Knowing all this, we can claim as truth that in everything—even our pain, hurt, sorrow, and suffering—God works for the good of those who love Him (Romans 8:28). There is redemption in our brokenness. We can believe the words of Paul in 2 Corinthians 4:16–18, "Therefore we do not lose heart. Though outwardly we are wasting away, yet inwardly we are being renewed day by day. For light and momentary troubles are achieving for us an external glory that far outweighs them all. So we fix our eyes not on what is seen, but on what is unseen, since what is seen is temporary, but what is unseen is eternal." And the joy we can feel in our hearts and souls happens in direct response to the goodness and love of our God.

Hebrews 11:1 says, "Now faith is confidence in what we hope for and assurance about what we do not see." If we trust in God's love for us and believe in His promise of eternal life, we have joy for today and hope for our future. These are gifts and blessings from God, and He wants us to claim them. John 15:11 says, "I have told you this so that my joy may be in you and that your joy may be complete." God has signed His signature in our lives and on our hearts, so we can't miss Him. He reveals His character to us, shows us His grace and goodness, and tells us who He is so that His joy can literally be within us and our joy will be complete.

The Divine Paradox

In giving we receive.
In loving we are loved.
In losing we gain.
In surrender we are victorious.
In dying we are born.
In forgiving we are forgiven.
In accepting we are accepted.
In death we find life.
In weakness we find strength.
In quiet we find music.
In letting go we are saved.
In pain we are healed.
In suffering we are restored.
In brokenness we are mended.
In pruning we grow.
In emptying we are filled.
In submission we find power.
In darkness we find light.
In mystery we find understanding.
In stillness we find God.
In *losing our life* we find *The Life*.
In the *paradox of faith* we are *transformed*.

—*Rhonda Dawes Milner*

Final Thoughts

*For God so loved the world that he gave his one
and only Son, that whoever believes in him
shall not perish but have eternal life.*

JOHN 3:16

GOD HOLDS NOTHING BACK FROM LOVING US. SOMETIMES
He shows us His love through small, simple things in creation, things
we've seen thousands of times before but overlooked. Other times, He
gets our attention in bigger ways, and we might wonder how we haven't
noticed Him there all along. I believe God has always revealed His love
for us in innumerable ways.

He speaks to us through nature. He reveals His magnificence in the
universe. He builds order into the world around us. His signature is
everywhere, including in us. The fact that we're here proves we're part of
His grand design.

He also makes Himself known through His Word and His Holy
Spirit. Throughout the Bible are passages with specific testimony of
God communicating to us through skies, ocean waves, breezes rustling
through the trees, fields, flowers, even birds that sing cheerfully. His Holy

Spirit helps us to discern truths about God in creation through our conscience and in other ways that resonate with our heart and mind. When
we experience and interact with His creation, something in our soul recognizes the truth.

God's creation is miraculous and amazing. And when we contemplate the intricacy of the world He's made, the mysteries of the universe,
the marvels of science, the design of the human body, or the signs of His
faithfulness in our lives, we see His glory. Everything He's created points
to an incredible master plan to reveal who He is and what He's about. He
sustains it all with power, wisdom, and goodness, and I believe He allows
us to receive hope, peace, and help through the wonders of His grand
design. He signs all it with His signature, so we have the opportunity to
know Him and live out the legacy for which we were created.

Romans 1:20 tells us, "For since the creation of the world God's
invisible qualities—his eternal power and divine nature—have been
clearly seen, being understood from what has been made, so that people
are without excuse." God doesn't want us to miss Him or to miss the
point of our lives. He's designed us each uniquely for a life of joy, faith,
and meaning. He uses all of creation to bless us, show us He's there, and
pursue a relationship with us.

When an artist creates something, their work reveals a lot about who
they are. I believe that as we look at a work of art, observing its mastery
of composition, skillfulness of strokes, thoughtfulness of details, or intricacy of design, we are able to appreciate it with different eyes. When we
look at, observe, and study the mastery, skillfulness, thoughtfulness, and
intricacy of our world and personal circumstances as created by God, we
notice that the mundane suddenly becomes profound; we see something
more than what we'd previously thought was there, and amazingly, something of the mystery of our existence becomes more clear. When we look
with different eyes, we are able to see beyond the expected and find the

unexpected, a world of intricate design and beauty, full and overflowing with meaning and significance. As we do this, we begin to sense and understand that we are a part of something that is so much bigger than we are, and we begin to see something of the magnificent glory that we are a part of in this world.

I believe God wants us—His creation—to understand our significance. Each one of us is cherished and beloved, an integral part of the great story of God's plan for humankind. Since we are created in His image, by knowing more about Him, we find out more about ourselves, our possibilities, and our potential. This allows us to transcend our regular situations, understand we're made for more, and have a different sense of who we are and what our purpose is.

God's creation is marked by His love. Nature, the universe, humankind, and the way He interacts with us through these reveal how He feels about us. His heart and His goodness have been built into all of it. Even more than signing His name for us to notice, He sent us His Son Jesus to make sure we wouldn't be lost. Colossians 1:17 says, "He is before all things, and in him all things hold together." Everything—creation, our lives, our circumstances, our future—is held together by Jesus, the one who came to give up His life for us. In Jesus, everything important is wrapped up in the only One in the universe powerful enough to save us. For me, the realization of who Jesus is and what He's done for me makes me feel humbled and incredibly loved. It moves me in my soul, provokes a response of gratefulness and joy, and compels me to love Him back.

Revelation 4:11 (NASB) says, "Worthy are You, our Lord and our God, to receive glory and honor and power; for You created all things, and because of Your will they existed, and were created." To me, God, the Creator of the Universe, my Maker, the One who loves me more than anyone, is more than worthy of all my sincerest praise and thanks. There is no one and no thing in all the world able to do what He did. He is awe-inspiring, glorious, powerful, holy, and good. Revelation 5:13 reads, "Then I heard every creature in heaven and on earth and under the earth and on the sea, and all that is in them, saying: 'To him who sits on the throne and to the Lamb be praise and honor and glory and power, for ever and ever!'" We—including every one of God's creatures—can't help but to respond to Him in praise when we realize who He is and what He's done. When our minds turn to all He's done for us, I pray our hearts turn to Him in worship and praise. And I pray this is where we find the deepest of blessings in our lives.

The thirteen chapters in this book have described qualities about God's character that I believe He wants us to know about Him. They offer my thoughts, heart, reflections, and studies—the journey I've been on as a Christian—and I pray you have been touched to see some of the countless ways in which God reveals His love to you through His creation. To be honest, though, His love is greater than I've been able to describe. Even here, at the conclusion of the book, I recognize that with all the incredible truths about God I've shared, these truths can still never come close to expressing the greatness of all of who He is. The God of creation is matchless and amazing. He cannot be understood with mere words.

And yet, He gives us Himself, so we can know Him. He offers us a context through which we might be able to see Him and find His love. Our universe holds together because God holds it together. God makes the rain fall, the wind blow, and the mountains move. He holds sub-atomic particles together and forms new life. He keeps all the systems of our body miraculously working. You can see His signature everywhere. Does this cause you to marvel? Is there something in your soul that recognizes He is who He says He is? Do you want to love Him back?

Responding to God's Signature

I believe the fact that you're holding this book in your hands is no accident. God has always been trying to get your attention through the ways He's shaped and engineered the circumstances of your life and surroundings. You may have noticed God's signature on things around you for some time but not necessarily known what to do with it all. The premise of this book is that God's creation reveals who He is and how He feels about you. He created you to know Him and has always pursued you with His love. Do you believe He loves you? And do you want to love Him back?

Matthew 6:33 tells us, "But seek first His kingdom and his righteousness, and all these things will be given to you as well." Matthew 7:7–8 says, "Ask and it will be given to you; seek and you will find; knock and the door will be opened to you. For everyone who asks receives; the one who seeks finds; and to the one who knocks, the door will be opened." If you want to find God, you can simply ask Him into your life. It might sound too easy, but the fact is, He already knows who you are, and you have already been found in Him. To live a life for Him, just open your heart to Him; He promises that if you ask, you will receive—a relationship with Him will be given to you, and He is already there, waiting to open the door to you.

To have a personal relationship with Him, we need to invite Him into our life. When we do this, we tell Him we're not perfect and know we're sinners in this fallen world; we acknowledge that Jesus died to take our sins away, and when He rose again, there's no condemnation for us anymore and we can have everlasting joy. When we accept Jesus Christ as the Savior of our lives, the Bible tells us that we are made new in Him and can now live the lives we were always meant to live.

Ephesians 4:22–24 says, "You were taught, with regard to your former way of life, to put off your old self, which is being corrupted by its deceitful desires; to be made new in the attitude of your minds; and to put on the new self, created to be like God in true righteousness and holiness." When we ask Jesus into our hearts and lives, all our sins—past, present, and future—are taken away in forgiveness. We become transformed and begin a journey of walking with Christ. This doesn't mean everything in us is magically different in an instant, but it acknowledges that something supernatural takes place in us, and we begin a process of transformation into becoming the child of God that He created us to be. We're still who we are, and even as we are imperfect on this side of Heaven, we know our sins are forgiven, and we can claim our new identity in Him as His beloved children. And as we love Him, everything about our being and existence becomes more clear; our heart desires to follow Jesus and become close to Him, the Holy Spirit opens our mind to God's words in Scripture so that we can better see and understand Him, and we become the best version of ourselves, which the Bible says happens when we are more conformed to the image of Christ.

Jesus tells us in Matthew 13:31–32 that "the kingdom of heaven is like a mustard seed, which a man took and planted in his field. Though it is the smallest of all seeds, yet when it grows, it is the largest of garden plants and becomes a tree, so that the birds come and perch on its branches." When we accept Jesus into our life, the kingdom of Heaven is like a mustard seed that has been planted in our hearts. The mustard seed starts out as the tiniest of seeds, but when it grows, it flourishes, becoming a tree so large that it's strong, able to offer blessings to others, and has a presence that reveals God's love, care, and interaction. As we grow in our faith, things of the world that used to fill our minds or consume our appetites often no longer have the same attraction. Things that used to upset us and cause worry, fear, stress, or anxiety are put in perspective. We have peace, strength, hope, resilience, patience, trust. We believe that God knows what is best for us and that He will care for us as a loving Father.

I encourage you to invite Christ into your life now and accept God's invitation to have eternal life with Him. It will be the best decision you ever made. You'll know how to have peace beyond understanding, experience calmness in your heart, give love without expectation, and live a life of joy and purpose. Asking Christ to be your Savior will literally save your life. No matter what journey you've been on so far in life and what things you think you've done, no sin is a surprise to God or too big for Him to forgive when you are truly repentant and desire forgiveness. Remember that He made you special and unique and has a special place for you—specially designed for you—in His Kingdom. His will for you is to be with Him for eternity and to become the person that He created you to be.

If this is what you desire for your life, tell Him and ask Him to come into your life. You are a child of God born of His love and brilliant design. Your destiny is to be His, forever and ever. He's shown you who He is in creation and in your life, and He's ready to receive you with love. Are you ready to respond to Him and invite Him into your heart?

A Prayer for the Ephesians

For this reason I kneel before the Father, from whom every family in heaven and on earth derives its name. I pray that out of his glorious riches He may strengthen you with power through his Spirit in your inner being, so that Christ may dwell in your hearts through faith. And I pray that you, being rooted and established in love, may have power, together with all the Lord's holy people, to grasp how wide and long and high and deep is the love of Christ, and to know this love that surpasses knowledge—that you may be filled to the measure of all the fullness of God.

Now to him who is able to do immeasurably more than all we ask or imagine, according to his power that is at work within us, to him be glory in the church and in Christ Jesus throughout all generations, for ever and ever! Amen.

—Ephesians 3:14–21

Acknowledgments

I'M GRATEFUL TO MY GRANDMOTHER, CLEO REDMOND Dawes, Nannie to me, who inspired me with her beautiful, unfaltering faith; Dr. Kenneth Boa, who has fostered my spiritual growth and development through the years; my sisters in Christ from my original prayer group: Lisa, Margie, Mary Jane, and Suzanne, who have helped me stay Christ-centered through their own faithfulness and devoted prayer; and the Richmont Graduate University faculty, staff, and students, who have witnessed to me the power of the Body of Christ and what it can accomplish. I am grateful to my husband for all of his support of my writings. I must also mention Britt, who has been at the core of my ministry, assisting me with her talents and skills.

I am exceedingly appreciative of the staff at Greenleaf Book Group for their efforts in the production of this book. I would like to single out Jessica Choi for her tireless work in editing; her beautiful Christian faith and words have enhanced my writing. As with my first book with Greenleaf Book Group, *The Mended Heart: A Poet's Journey Through Love, Suffering, and Hope,* my second published book has exceeded all my hopes and expectations.

This book is also a thank-you to God for the life of my son, Whitner, who died on April 17, 2011, shortly after the completion of my preliminary manuscript. He was able to read my writing, so I am thankful for that. We were graced with his presence for twenty-five years and blessed to see him become an amazing young man of faith. I know he watches over me constantly, as I need a lot of care and guidance as a wandering but not lost sheep. I must add once again that he died in our family pool from practicing breath-holding for a spearfishing trip. I founded an organization called Shallow Water Blackout Prevention to raise awareness of and educate people on the dangers of underwater breath-holding. Please visit www.shallowwaterblackoutprevention.org to learn more.

My deepest thanks go to God, who has shaped every circumstance of my life—both easy and hard, beautiful and heartbreaking—to show me His love and lead me down this path of my life. He is always the encouraging voice behind me.

> *"Whether you turn to the right or to the left, your ears will hear a voice behind you, saying, 'This is the way; walk in it.'"*
>
> ISAIAH 30:21

Notes

Preface

1. For a discussion on this, see C. S. Lewis, *Mere Christianity* (New York: Macmillan Publishing, 1952), 41; and Josh McDowell, *More Than a Carpenter* (Wheaton, IL: Tyndale House Publishers, 1977), 25–35.

Introduction: God's Signature

1. Ken Boa and Larry Moody, *I'm Glad You Asked* (Colorado Springs, CO: Victor, 2005), 177.

Chapter Two: God's Existence and Constancy

1. Patrick Glynn, *God: The Evidence* (New York: Three Rivers Press, 1999), 21–55.

2. Ibid., 21–55.

3. Hugh Ross, *More Than a Theory* (Grand Rapids, MI: Baker Books, 2009), 95–98.

4. Hugh Ross, *Creation as Science* (Colorado Springs, CO: NavPress, 2006), 86.

5. Javier Leach, *Mathematics and Religion* (West Conshohocken, PA: Templeton Press, 2010), 22.

6. Brian Greene, *The Elegant Universe: Superstrings, Hidden Dimensions, and the Quest for the Ultimate Theory* (New York: W. W. Norton, 1999).

7. Nick Herbert, *Quantum Reality: Beyond the New Physics* (New York: Anchor Books, 1985).

8. Gustaf Stromberg, "Coherence in the Physical World." *Philosophy of Science*, 9 (1942), 323-34.

9. Glynn, 21–55.

10. Ross, *Creation as Science*, 90–2.

11. Glynn, 21–55.

Chapter Three: God's Intelligence and Genius

1. Francis Collins, *The Language of God* (New York: Free Press, 2006), 106–7.

Chapter Four: God's Power and Strength

1. Hannah Hurnard, *Hinds' Feet on High Places* (Wheaton, IL: Tyndale House Publishers, 1986), 253.

2. St. Augustine, *The Confessions*, trans. Henry Chadwick (Oxford, England: Oxford University Press, 1991), 3.

Chapter Five: God's Comfort and Presence

1. A. W. Tozer, *The Pursuit of God* (Camp Hill, PA: Christian Publications, 1995), 15.

2. C. S. Lewis, *The Problem of Pain* (New York: Touchstone, 1996), 83.

3. Iain Matthew, *The Impact of God* (Great Britain: Hodder and Stoughton, 1995), 92–93.

Chapter Six: God's Glory and Majesty

1. Katherine Lee Bates (lyrics) and Samuel Ward (music), "America the Beautiful," 1913.

Chapter Seven: God's Miracles and Creativity

1. Doris Stickney, *Water Bugs and Dragonflies* (New York: Pilgrim Press, 1982), 3–14.

Chapter Eight: God's Mystery and Omniscience

1. C. Stephen Evans, *Søren Kierkegaard's Christian Psychology* (Vancouver, British Columbia: Regent College Publishing, 1990), 53–56.

2. C. S. Lewis, *The Problem of Pain* (New York: Touchstone, 1996), 88–89, 103.

3. Terry D. Cooper, *Dimensions of Evil* (Minneapolis, MN: Fortress Press, 2007), 225–226.

4. Evans, *Kierkegaard's Christian Psychology*, 50.

Chapter Nine: God's Truth and Wisdom

1. C. S. Lewis, *Mere Christianity* (New York: Macmillan Publishing, 1952), 3–16.

2. Harold Koenig, *Medicine, Religion, and Health* (West Conshohocken, PA: Templeton Foundation Press, 2008), 3–4, 82–95, 129–145, 111–128.

Chapter Ten: God's Love and Acceptance

1. Iain Matthew, *The Impact of God* (Great Britain: Hodder and Stoughton, 1995), 25-27

2. Robert R. Perkinson, *Chemical Dependency Counseling* (Los Angeles, CA: Sage Publications, 2008), 130–131.

3. C. S. Lewis, *The Weight of Glory and Other Addresses* (New York: Touchstone, 1980), 28–29.

4. James Bryan Smith, *The Good and Beautiful Life* (Westmont, IL: IVP Books, 2010), 94.

5. Gerald May, *Addiction and Grace* (New York: HarperCollins, 1988), 30.

Chapter Eleven: God's Grace and Mercy

1. George MacDonald, Michael Phillips (ed.), *Your Life in Christ* (Bloomington, MN: Bethany House, 2005), 169–173.

2. Dallas Willard, *The Spirit of the Disciplines* (New York: HarperCollins, 1988), 9.

3. Brother Lawrence, *The Practice of the Presence of God* (Grand Rapids, MI: Spire Books, 1967), 95.

About the Author

Rhonda Dawes Milner, MD, MA, LPC, is a native Atlantan who resides primarily in her hometown with her husband and six dogs. She has seen her four children into adulthood.

She graduated *summa cum laude* from the University of Georgia in 1976 with a BS in microbiology. At the University of Georgia she was elected to Phi Beta Kappa and was the first woman ever elected to ODK (Omicron Delta Kappa), the National Leadership Honor Society.

Rhonda graduated from Emory University School of Medicine in 1980 with an MD and was elected to Who's Who in American Colleges and Universities. She went on to do her residency in radiology at the Emory University Affiliated Hospitals and is a board-certified radiologist. She was in private practice for eight and a half years, then received a clinical appointment at Grady Memorial Hospital, an Emory Affiliated Hospital, where she volunteered with the residents, teaching mammography for five years.

She retired to spend time with her husband and four children. As an empty-nester, she returned to graduate school, this time receiving two master's degrees, one in professional counseling and the other in ministry, from Richmont Graduate University (RGU) in Atlanta, Georgia. She specialized in addiction and also spirituality and counseling, and has a certificate as a trained spiritual director from RGU. In addition, she trained under the late Dallas Willard, Kenneth Boa, and Gary Moon at the Renovaré Institute, where she received a certificate in Spiritual Formation and Discipleship.

Rhonda is a bereaved parent who has suffered the pain and anguish of great loss and tragedy. She also knows personally, in her family, of the kind of life-threatening addiction that robs people of joy and life. But she believes that God does not waste any experience. She mentions in this book some of her supernatural experiences or "God Kisses" that she has had since her son's death. She has written many more stories about them, as they continue in her life as gifts from Heaven, and they can be read on her website, www.healingpresenceministry.com, under "Afterlife Kisses."

Rhonda looks back on her twenties as a time when she stretched herself intellectually during college, medical school, and residency; her thirties and early forties as a time when she stretched herself emotionally by raising four children born within a five-year time span, all of them with ADHD; and her late forties and early fifties as a time when she stretched herself physically by running two marathons and hiking the Inca trail from Cuzco to Machu Picchu in Peru. In her mid-fifties and early sixties, she has stretched herself with her spiritual and psychological studies and is now primarily focused on her spiritual journey. Her first book, *The Mended Heart: A Poet's Journey though Love, Suffering, and Hope*, is an Amazon bestseller composed of her poetry, spiritual writings, and photography.

The Signature of God is her first book of reflections on and apologetics for God. She wrote it for you and to speak the truth of God, knowing that He speaks to us, His own creation, through His creation. He has signed His name on all of us, as we are all His beloved.

Twenty percent of all profits from the sale of this book will go toward spreading God's love through Healing Presence Ministry, saving lives through Shallow Water Blackout Prevention, opioid addition prevention and treatment, and mental illness awareness and treatment.